Headway

Culture and Literature Companion
Intermediate (B1+)

Peter May

OXFORD
UNIVERSITY PRESS

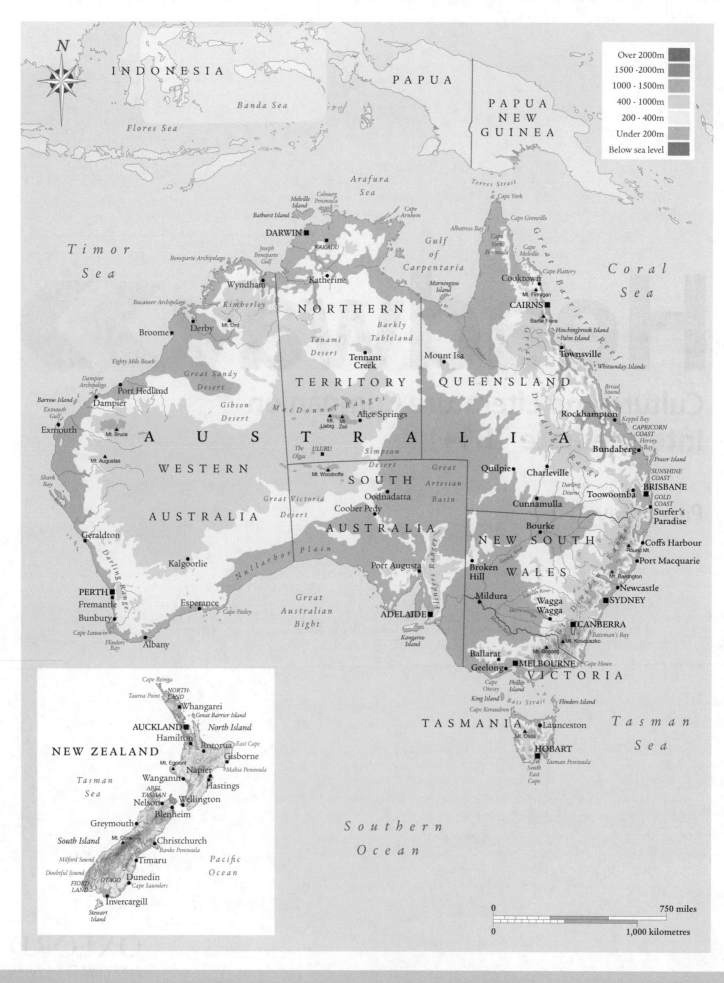

INDONESIA

Banda Sea

Flores Sea

PAPUA

PAPUA NEW GUINEA

Timor Sea

Arafura Sea

Gulf of Carpentaria

Coral Sea

Over 2000m
1500 - 2000m
1000 - 1500m
400 - 1000m
200 - 400m
Under 200m
Below sea level

Torres Strait
Cape York

Melville Island
Bathurst Island
Cobourg Peninsula
Cape Arnhem
Cape Grenville
Albatross Bay

DARWIN
KAKADU
Joseph Bonaparte Gulf

Cape York *Peninsula*
Cape Melville
Cooktown
Mt. Finnigan
Cape Flattery

Wyndham
Katherine
Mornington Island
CAIRNS
Bartle Frere

Bonaparte Archipelago
Bucaneer Archipelago
Kimberley
Mt. Ord

NORTHERN

Barkly Tableland
Mount Isa
Hinchinbrook Island
Palm Island
Townsville
Whitsunday Islands

Broome
Derby

Eighty Mile Beach

Tanami Desert

TERRITORY

QUEENSLAND

Dividing
Broad Sound

Dampier Archipelago
Barrow Island
Port Hedland
Dampier

Great Sandy Desert

Tennant Creek

Rockhampton
Keppel Bay
CAPRICORN COAST
Hervey Bay

Exmouth Gulf
Exmouth

Gibson Desert

MacDonnel   *Ranges*
Alice Springs

Bundaberg
Fraser Island

Mt. Bruce

Shark Bay

Mt. Augustas

A U S T R A L I A

The Olgas *ULURU*
Mt. Liebig Mt. Zeil
Mt. Woodroffe

Simpson Desert

Great Artesian Basin

SUNSHINE COAST

WESTERN

Quilpie
Charleville
Darling Downs
Toowoomba
BRISBANE
GOLD COAST
Surfer's Paradise

AUSTRALIA

Great Victoria Desert

SOUTH

Oodnadatta
Coober Pedy

AUSTRALIA

Cunnamulla

NEW SOUTH

Coffs Harbour
Round Mt.
Port Macquarie

Geraldton

Darling Ranges

Nullarbor Plain

Port Augusta

Bourke

Darling River

WALES
Mt. Barrington

Kalgoorlie

Broken Hill

Newcastle
SYDNEY

PERTH
Fremantle
Bunbury

Esperance
Cape Pasley

Great Australian Bight

Mildura
Wagga Wagga

CANBERRA
Bateman's Bay
Mt. Kosciuszko

Cape Leeuwin
Flinders Bay
Albany

ADELAIDE

Flinders Ranges

Murray River
Murrumbidgee River

Ballarat
Geelong
MELBOURNE
Mt. Bogong
Cape Howe
VICTORIA

Kangaroo Island

Cape Otway *Phillip Island*
King Island *Bass Strait* *Flinders Island*
Cape Keraudren

Tasman Sea

TASMANIA
Mt. Ossa Launceston

HOBART
Tasman Peninsula
South East Cape

Southern Ocean

NEW ZEALAND

Cape Reinga
Tauroa Point
NORTH-LAND
Whangarei
Great Barrier Island
AUCKLAND
North Island
Hamilton
Rotorua
East Cape
Gisborne
Mt. Egmont
Napier
Mahia Peninsula
Wanganui
Hastings
ABEL TASMAN
Nelson
Wellington
Blenheim

Tasman Sea

Greymouth

South Island
Mt. Cook
Canterbury Plain
Christchurch
Banks Peninsula
Milford Sound
Timaru
Doubtful Sound
FIORD LAND
OTAGO
Dunedin
Cape Saunders
Invercargill
Stewart Island

Pacific Ocean

0   750 miles

0   1,000 kilometres

Contents

1A

The British Empire

1 In past centuries, European countries took control of, or *colonized*, other parts of the world. These *colonies* included Australia (colonized by Britain), Algeria (France) and Argentina (Spain). Match these countries to their former colonies.

1	Belgium	a	Senegal
2	Holland	b	India
3	Portugal	c	Brazil
4	France	d	Indonesia
5	Spain	e	Congo
6	Britain	f	Mexico

2 Look at the title of the article. What do you think it means? Read the text quickly and match paragraphs 1–6 with summaries a–f.

a ☐ The gradual fall of the Empire
b ☐ The early history of the Empire
c ☐ The present-day legacy of the Empire
d ☐ The size and reach of the Empire
e ☐ The effects of the Empire on the colonies
f ☐ The private company which ran part of the Empire

The sun never set …

1 No country has ever ruled over the entire planet, but the British have come the closest. The British Empire was the largest in history. By 1921, approximately one quarter of the world's population was part of the British Empire, and its power and influence extended to every continent. At its peak, it covered so much of the surface of the Earth that it was literally true that the sun never set on it. It was always daylight somewhere in the Empire.

2 The Empire was expanded over hundreds of years by trade, settlement and conquest. In 1497, John Cabot, an Italian mariner sponsored by King Henry VII, landed in Newfoundland and made it an English overseas territory. During the reign of Queen Elizabeth I (1533–1603), the English navy became the most powerful in the world after defeating the Spanish navy (the Armada). In 1580, Sir Francis Drake – a key participant in that victory – was the first Englishman to circumnavigate the globe, and English colonization started. North America was first, including Canada and Caribbean islands like Jamaica and Barbados. Although Dutch explorers visited Australia in the 17th century, it was the English who first settled there, starting with penal colonies. This was followed by the colonization of New Zealand.

3 In the East, Britain's Asian empire was established by the British East India Company. It became extremely powerful during the 17th and 18th centuries, and by the 1850s the company had grown from a commercial trading organization to one which virtually ruled India. It even had its own army and fought many wars with local Indian rulers during its conquest of the country. The British crown took control of the company in 1858.

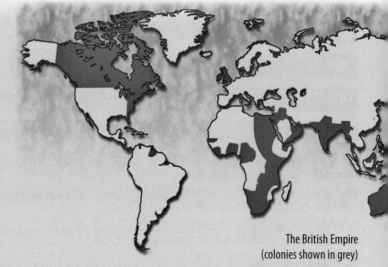

The British Empire
(colonies shown in grey)

4 It can be argued that the colonies benefited from British occupation in several ways: the form of government, the legal system, the English language – even sports such as football, rugby and cricket. However, the colonies also suffered under British rule: many developed only as raw materials suppliers of crops such as sugar and cotton, to satisfy Britain's trading interests. This meant they were dangerously reliant on harvests and economic conditions. The British also committed terrible atrocities in some countries, and transported across the Atlantic millions of African slaves, many of whom died during the journey. The slave trade was finally made illegal in Britain in 1807, and abolished throughout the Empire in 1834.

5 Despite its continuing physical expansion in the 19th century, above all in Africa, the Empire had actually begun to decline in the previous century, especially after the American War of Independence. Canada and Australia became self-governing colonies in the 1840s and 1850s, India finally became independent in 1947, and after that nearly all of Britain's other colonies followed over the next two decades.

3 Read the article and answer the questions.

1 How many people lived in the Empire in 1921?
2 What made England stronger during the Elizabethan era?
3 Who were the first Europeans to reach Australia?
4 What was unusual about the British East India Company?
5 What were the positive and negative aspects of British influence on the colonies?
6 Which event helped start the decline of the Empire?
7 What is the Commonwealth?
8 Which European country says a British colony is part of its territory?

The Queen Victoria Memorial, Calcutta

6 However, most of the former British colonies still remain linked through the Commonwealth of Nations, an association of 53 independent countries. Britain, like other ex-imperial powers, still has control of a number of small overseas territories. These include islands in the Caribbean, South Atlantic and elsewhere. In the cases of the Falkland Islands and Gibraltar, there are disputes with neighbouring countries – Argentina and Spain respectively – over sovereignty.

4 Match these words from the text with meanings a–l.

1	conquest		7	slave trade	
2	sponsored		8	abolished	
3	overseas territory		9	raw materials	
4	reign		10	atrocities	
5	circumnavigate		11	decline	
6	settled		12	sovereignty	

a natural products, often used to manufacture things
b area of land belonging to a distant country
c went to live permanently
d to get smaller
e acts of extreme cruelty
f period when a king or queen ruled a country
g ownership of an area of land (by a country)
h taking control by force
i buying and selling people, and forcing them to work
j given money
k go completely around, in a ship
l ended, by law

What do you think?

- How do you think people in those countries felt when Europeans colonized them? How would you feel if a powerful nation conquered and colonized your country?
- Can it ever be right for one country to colonize another? Should a country keep an overseas territory forever if the people who have settled there want it to? What if another country claims that territory?

PROJECT

Choose a former British colony and write a short FactFile about it. Use the Internet and/or books to find details about it. Include information on:
- when and how it became a British colony
- what effects colonization had on it
- when and how it became independent
- what the country is like now

1 Nowadays, most countries have large populations of people who came – or whose families came – from other parts of the world. Where have immigrants to your country mostly come from? What language(s) do immigrants in your country usually speak a) at home? b) at school or work? c) in their social life? Why? What do you think it's like to use different languages in this way?

2 Read the text about the poet Sujata Bhatt and complete the notes.

Sujata Bhatt

Sujata Bhatt was born in 1956 and grew up in the Indian city of Pune, sometimes called the 'Oxford of the East' owing to its famous educational institutions, but emigrated with her family to the United States in 1968. Since then, Sujata has lived in a number of different places including Canada, where she was Writer in Residence at the University of Victoria. She currently lives in Bremen, Germany, and in 2013 was made Visiting Professor of Creative Writing at Nottingham Trent University in the UK.

Her first collection, *Brunizem*, won the Commonwealth Poetry Prize (Asia) and the Alice Hunt Bartlett Award. Subsequent collections have been awarded a Poetry Book Society Recommendation and in 1991 she received a Cholmondeley Award.

For Bhatt, language is synonymous with the tongue, the physical act of speaking. She has described the Gujarati language and the Indian childhood it connects her to as 'the deepest layer of my identity'. However, English has become the language she speaks at home and which she, largely, chooses to write in. The repercussions of this divided heritage are explored in her work, most explicitly in 'Search for My Tongue', which alternates between the two languages.

The complex status of English – its beauty and colonial implications – are also conveyed in the moving ironies of her poem 'A Different History', a set text in the 2015 Cambridge English Literature IGCSE Examination. Her cultural heritage is present too in her voice, with its musical synthesis of Indian and American inflections.

FACTFILE

▶ Born: ____1956____

▶ Childhood in Pune, in [1]_____

▶ Countries also lived in: [2]_____ , [3]_____ , [4]_____

▶ Main languages spoken: [5]_____ and [6]_____

▶ Poetry reflects her [7]_____ from two different cultures.

▶ Her poem [8]_____ used in Cambridge IGCSE.

▶ Dual cultural background also heard in her [9]_____

3 Read Sujata Bhatt's *Search for My Tongue*. Then match the three sections of the poem with summaries **A–C**.

A She is sure that her first language will always be part of her.

B She thinks she's lost her first language completely.

C She finds, while she is dreaming, that her first language is still with her.

Search for My Tongue

¹ You ask me what I mean
by saying I have lost my tongue.
I ask you, what would you do
if you had two tongues in your mouth,
and lost the first one, the mother tongue,
and could not really know the other,
the foreign tongue.
You could not use them both together
even if you thought that way.
And if you lived in a place you had to
speak a foreign tongue,
your mother tongue would rot,
rot and die in your mouth
until you had to spit it out.
I thought I spit it out
but overnight while I dream,

² મને હતું કે આખ્ખી જીબ આખ્ખી ભાષા,
(munay hutoo kay aakhee jeebh aakhee bhasha)

મેં થૂં કી નાખી છે.
(may thoonky nakhi chay)

પરંતુ રાત્રે સ્વપ્નામાં મારી ભાષા પાછી આવે છે.
(parantoo rattray svupnama mari bhasha pachi aavay chay)

ફૂલની જેમ મારી ભાષા મારી જીબ
(foolnee jaim mari bhasha nmari jeebh)

મોઢામાં ખીલે છે.
(modhama kheelay chay)

ફૂલની જેમ મારી ભાષા મારી જીબ
(fullnee jaim mari bhasha mari jeebh)

મોઢામાં પાકે છે.
(modhama pakay chay)

³ it grows back, a stump of a shoot
grows longer, grows moist, grows strong veins,
it ties the other tongue in knots,
the bud opens, the bud opens in my mouth,
it pushes the other tongue aside.
Everytime I think I've forgotten,
I think I've lost the mother tongue,
it blossoms out of my mouth.

4 Answer the questions about *Search for My Tongue*.

1 What do these expressions using the word 'tongue' usually mean?
   lose your tongue / mother tongue / foreign tongue
   Is she using the word 'tongue' here literally or metaphorically?

2 What is meant here by having 'two tongues in your mouth'?

3 What does she fear might happen to her first language? Why? What metaphors does she use in the first section to describe this? What does this suggest the experience feels like?

4 Read the second section aloud (the way it sounds to an English speaker is given in brackets). Why do you think this section of the poem is translated into English sounds? Why do you think the poet has included the lines in Gujarati?

5 In the third section, what is used as a metaphor for the tongue? Which words are used to illustrate this? What do they mean?

6 In what tone do you think the third section of the poem should be read? Why?

7 Does the poem have a rhyme scheme, or a special rhythm? What kind of English does the poem use? Why do you think is it written this way?

What do you think?

- If you lived in a different country for a long time, do you think you could learn to speak the new language as confidently as you speak your first language? Why? / Why not?
- Do you think you would start to lose your first language, and if so, how would you feel about that? What could you do to preserve it?
- What would you miss most if you went to live in a different culture, and why? Is it possible to be completely bi-cultural, or does integrating into another society inevitably lead to losing part of your cultural identity?

PROJECT

Choose somebody famous in your country who also has a cultural heritage from another part of the world. Find out more about them and write an article for a school magazine. Include information about:

- where they were born and grew up
- the main differences between that culture and where they live now
- what they do and how those differences have influenced their work and life

1 Look at these two photos of BBC TV studios. When do you think each was taken? What differences are there?

2 What is 'BBC English'? Where does the BBC get its money from? Is its reporting impartial or does it only express government opinions? Read the text to check your answers.

The BBC

At 6 p.m. on 14 November 1922, a short news bulletin announced the arrival of what was to become the world's biggest broadcaster: the British Broadcasting Corporation, better known as the BBC. Then, as now, its mission was to 'educate, inform and entertain', initially by live radio transmissions of events such as classical music concerts, drama and sport, plus regular news updates and weather forecasts. In 1932 it began to reach an international audience through the BBC World Service, which nowadays broadcasts in 28 languages to an estimated 192 million listeners worldwide, with plans to extend this to 39 languages and an audience of half a billion very soon.

BBC television was launched in 1936, and the number of viewers gradually increased after the Second World War. At that time the term 'BBC English' was sometimes used to mean the standard form of pronunciation in Southern England, as used by nearly all the early broadcasters. But once the Corporation's monopoly of British television was ended in 1955 by the appearance of ITV, its first commercial rival, the nature of its programmes began to change and so did many of the accents of those appearing on the BBC, reflecting the diversity of people in the UK.

From that time on, BBC Television has broadcast an increasingly wide range of programmes, from chat shows, sitcoms and soaps to consumer shows, costume dramas and current affairs programmes. Wildlife documentaries such as those made by David Attenborough and long-running series like *Dr Who* have become popular in many countries. BBC Online, now bbc.com, was launched in 1997 and has since become one of the world's most popular websites.

The BBC is a public corporation independent from government. It has never carried advertising and is financed partly by the sale of programmes abroad, but mainly by an annual licence fee of around £150 which must be paid by every British household that receives broadcast television via a TV, computer or mobile phone. Non-payment is a criminal offence which results in over 150,000 prosecutions every year.

This method of funding is unpopular with both the growing number of people who have to a buy a TV licence even though – with hundreds of other channels now available – they may rarely, if ever, watch or listen to the BBC, and also with rival media organizations that consider the annual £4 billion provided by the licence fee to be a form of unfair competition.

Despite the BBC's commitment to impartiality, its reporting has also attracted criticism, both from the Left for allegedly being 'monarchist', 'pro-business' or 'unionist', for instance in its coverage of the 2014 referendum on Scottish independence, and also from the Right for its supposed 'cultural liberal bias' when dealing with religion, social issues and – above all – political issues such as Brexit.

The BBC totally rejects these accusations, arguing that as it receives money neither from government nor advertisers, it is free from all political or commercial pressure. It reminds its critics that

3 Read the text again carefully. Are these statements True (**T**) or False (**F**)?

1 The BBC began showing TV programmes in 1922.
2 People who appear on BBC television always speak in an upper-class accent.
3 Some BBC TV shows have an international audience.
4 The British government runs the BBC.
5 There are no advertisements on BBC TV or radio.
6 Everybody in Britain is happy to pay for a TV licence.
7 Only very conservative people say the BBC's reporting is unfair.
8 The BBC believes that people still trust it to tell them the truth.
9 The series W1A is about real people who work at the BBC.
10 According to the text, W1A is an example of the BBC at its best.

4 Which types of TV programme are mentioned in the third paragraph? Explain the meaning of each. Which ones are shown in the pictures below?

even in an age where there are so many alternative sources of information, the majority of the British public still prefer to get their news from the BBC, particularly at times of great national events. It also points out that it is aware it has its faults, is constantly doing its best to deal with them and – unlike many other large organizations – is able to laugh at itself.

The satirical sitcom W1A, for instance, is actually set in the headquarters of the BBC, where a group of overpaid and over-promoted middle managers with job titles such as Head of Values and Director of Better have an endless series of meetings in which hopelessly impractical ideas are exchanged, invariably resulting in no action whatsoever. Those with inside knowledge of the Corporation admit the series is at times uncomfortably close to the reality, but the fact that the BBC is capable of making such a programme about itself seems to many a reflection of just how impartial it is – and what brilliant television it can still produce.

5 Match these words from the text with meanings a–l.

> broadcasting   mission   diversity   household
> offence   prosecution   funding   coverage
> bias   issues   satirical   impartial

a unfairness in reporting, showing favour to one side
b the process of being charged with a crime in court
c the work that the people in an organization believe it is their duty to do
d important topics that people are discussing
e providing money for a particular purpose
f range of things that are very different from each other
g not supporting one person or group more than another
h making and sending out radio or television programmes
i using humour to criticize someone or something
j illegal act
k the reporting of news in the media
l group of people, such as a family, who live together

What do you think?

- Would people in your country be happy to pay the equivalent of around £150 a year to watch the BBC?
- Do you prefer to watch TV with or without breaks for advertising? Why?
- Which provides more reliable news: public TV / radio, or private TV / radio channels?
- Have you ever watched the BBC news? If so, do you think it was biased or impartial? How does it compare to news channels in your country?
- Do families in your country still sit down together to watch TV in the evening? Why? / Why not?
- Do you think you watch too much TV and/or online entertainment? Why? / Why not?

PROJECT

Watch or listen to a BBC news bulletin on a TV channel such as BBC World or a radio station such as BBC World Service. Make notes on the following, and then write a review of the programme in 120–150 words.

- The time and length of the bulletin.
- The gender and approximate age of the newsreader and the reporters.
- How easy or difficult it was to understand.
- The countries and main topics covered.
- Whether you found the reporting biased or impartial, and why.

1 Elizabeth I was Queen of England in the late 16th century. She was one of the Tudors, a family that ruled England and Wales for 118 years. Do you know anything about her? What was happening in your country at that time?

2 Read the text and complete this extract from the royal family tree.

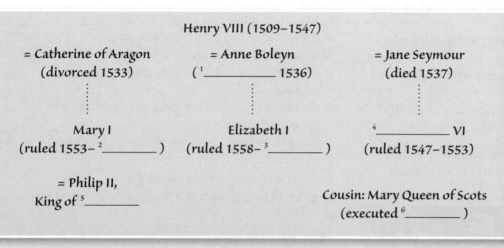

Henry VIII (1509–1547)

= Catherine of Aragon (divorced 1533)

= Anne Boleyn ([1]_____ 1536)

= Jane Seymour (died 1537)

Mary I (ruled 1553– [2]_____)

Elizabeth I (ruled 1558– [3]_____)

[4]_____ VI (ruled 1547–1553)

= Philip II, King of [5]_____

Cousin: Mary Queen of Scots (executed [6]_____)

Elizabeth I

[1] **ELIZABETH I**, the last Tudor monarch, was born at Greenwich on 7 September 1533, the daughter of Henry VIII and his second wife, Anne Boleyn, who was executed three years later.

[2] Her early life was full of uncertainties, and her chances of succeeding to the throne seemed very slight once her half-brother Edward was born in 1537. She was then third in line behind her Catholic half-sister, Mary. Edward became king in 1547, aged 9 (he was known as 'The Boy King'), but died in 1553, leaving Elizabeth second in line to the throne when Mary became queen. Catholics always mistrusted Elizabeth, and she only narrowly escaped execution following a failed rebellion in 1554 against Queen Mary, who had become very unpopular after marrying King Philip of Spain.

[3] Elizabeth succeeded to the throne on her half-sister's death in November 1558. She was very well-educated (fluent in six languages), and had inherited intelligence and determination from both parents.

[4] During her reign, a secure Church of England was established. Most of her subjects accepted a compromise between Catholicism and Protestantism as the basis of their faith, and this probably saved England from the kind of religious wars that France suffered from in the second half of the 16th century.

[5] Elizabeth's reign also saw many brave voyages of discovery, including those of Francis Drake, Walter Raleigh and Humphrey Gilbert, particularly to the Americas. These expeditions prepared England for an age of colonization and trade expansion.

[6] The arts flourished, too. Country houses such as Longleat and Hardwick Hall were built and theatres thrived – Queen Elizabeth attended the first performance of Shakespeare's *A Midsummer Night's Dream*.

[7] The image of Elizabeth's reign is one of triumph and success. The Queen herself was often called 'Gloriana', 'Good Queen Bess' and 'The Virgin Queen'. With her expensive clothes and jewellery (to look the part, like all sovereigns of the day), she cultivated this image by touring the country, often riding on horseback rather than by carriage. Elizabeth made at least 25 such tours during her reign.

[8] However, Elizabeth's reign was one of danger and difficulty for many, with threats of invasion from Spain through Ireland, and from France through Scotland. Much of northern England was in rebellion in 1569-70, and she passed harsh laws against Catholics after plots against her life were discovered.

3 Match the beginnings and the endings of the sentences.

1	Elizabeth seemed unlikely ever to become Queen	a	because lands had been discovered during Elizabeth's reign.
2	She eventually became Queen of England	b	because some people wanted to use her against Elizabeth.
3	In 16th century England there were no wars of religion	c	because Mary I had been his wife.
4	England later began to establish colonies	d	because both Edward VI and Mary I had died.
5	She travelled around dressed like a queen	e	because Elizabeth had spent a lot on wars.
6	Elizabeth was sometimes cruel to Catholics	f	because she was the youngest of three children.
7	Mary, Queen of Scots, was kept in prison	g	because she wanted to impress her subjects.
8	The King of Spain said he was also King of England	h	because few people were totally against the new faith.
9	The next English king had serious money problems	i	because having a husband could have been disastrous for her country.
10	Elizabeth decided to remain single all her life	j	because supporters of Philip II were trying to kill her.

9 One such plot involved her cousin Mary, Queen of Scots. As a likely successor to Elizabeth, Mary spent 19 years as Elizabeth's prisoner because Mary was the focus for rebellion and possible assassination plots. Mary was also a temptation for potential invaders such as Philip II of Spain, and in 1587 Mary was tried, found guilty and executed.

10 In 1588, aided by bad weather, the English navy scored a great victory over the Spanish invasion fleet of around 130 ships – the 'Armada'. The Armada's aim had been to overthrow the Queen and re-establish Catholicism by conquest, as Philip II believed he had a claim to the English throne through his marriage to Queen Mary I.

11 During Elizabeth's long reign, the nation also suffered from high prices and severe economic depression. Wars in France and against Spain, which included support for rebels against Philip II in the Spanish Netherlands (comprising much of modern Holland, Belgium and Luxembourg), were very costly. Elizabeth left large debts to her successor, James I.

12 Elizabeth used her marriage prospects as a political tool, both nationally and internationally, but she chose never to marry. If she had chosen a foreign prince, he would have drawn England into foreign policies for his own advantages (as in her sister Mary's marriage to Philip of Spain); marrying a fellow countryman could have drawn the Queen into disputes between powerful groups.

13 As a result, the 'Virgin Queen' was seen as a selfless woman who sacrificed personal happiness for the good of the nation, to which she was, in a way, 'married'. She seems to have been very popular with the majority of her subjects and, overall, Elizabeth's leadership brought successes during a period of great danger both at home and abroad. She died at Richmond Palace on 24 March 1603, having become a legend in her lifetime. The date of her accession was a national holiday for two hundred years. The number of films made about her life in recent years show that she has become a modern icon too, especially for women seeking to gain power at the highest levels of society.

4 Find words or phrases in the text that mean the following. The paragraph numbers are in brackets.

1 king or queen (1)
2 put to death (1)
3 becoming the next king or queen (2)
4 a fight against authority (2)
5 people of a country that has a king or queen (4)
6 kings or queens (7)
7 vehicle pulled by horses (7)
8 very hard or strict (8)
9 secret plans to kill somebody powerful (9)
10 remove a leader by force (10)
11 arguments (12)
12 becoming the king or queen (13)

What do you think?

- Do you think it was right for monarchs in those days to have so much power? What role does the royal family in your country have today? Do you think they are relevant to 21st century society? What are the advantages and disadvantages of having a royal family?

PROJECT

Look at the quote from Elizabeth I.

'I know I have the body of a weak, feeble woman; but I have the heart and stomach of a king ~ and of a King of England too.'

From a speech by Elizabeth I to her army at Tilbury (near London) on the eve of the battle against the Spanish Armada, 1588.

Choose another woman who had a powerful impact on history and find out as much as you can about her. Write an article for a history website about her background and achievements, saying why you think she should be included in their list of 'the top five female figures in history'.

1 What do the pictures show?
What sort of artist has created them?
What do you think each work means?

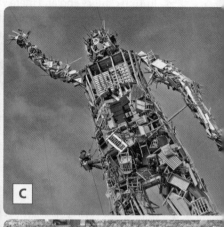

2 Read the text and match paragraphs 3–8 with the works in pictures A–F .

Sir Antony Gormley

Britain's most famous living sculptor

1 Antony Mark David Gormley was born on 30 August 1950 to a German mother and an Irish father. The youngest of seven children, Gormley grew up in Hampstead, London and did a degree in archaeology, anthropology and history of art at Trinity College, Cambridge. After graduating, he earned money by painting murals in night clubs. In 1971 he travelled to India and Sri Lanka, where he studied Buddhism – a journey which made a big impression on the young artist, and influenced many of his creative ideas.

2 When he returned to London in 1974, he studied many different kinds of art, before focusing on sculpture. Almost all of his work takes the human form as its subject, with Gormley trying to express the human body as a 'place', not a 'thing', and linking personal experience to all human beings – showing the collective nature of humanity.

3 In 1994 Gormley won the Turner Prize for **Field**, a collection of 35,000 terracotta human figures, each between 8 and 26 cm tall. The work gives the impression of a tide of humanity, an infinite mass that not only fills the part of the building housing the installation, but might well extend far beyond what we can actually see. When we look at the figures, they all seem to be staring at us, so that in a way *we* become the focus of the work, not them.

4 Unlike many other British artists, Gormley does not have many of his works in galleries. His most famous piece, **The Angel of the North**, is a 20-metre-high figure standing on a hilltop near Newcastle. On a site visible from the nearby busy A1 road, the angel reminds travellers of the industrial history of this region, including the coal miners who toiled away in the dark beneath the hill for two centuries. It also, according to the sculptor, represents the shift from the industrial era to the modern age of information technology.

5 **Another Place** features 100 cast-iron figures, made from moulds of Gormley's own body, standing on a three-kilometre stretch of beach near Liverpool. Each time the tide rises, the figures are submerged in 'another place' and then revealed by the water as the tide falls. The theme is also immigration and emigration, as the figures look out across the waves towards the Irish Sea and the Atlantic.

3 Which work of Gormley's … ?

1 was destroyed after it had been constructed
2 is about people going abroad to live
3 makes viewers feel they are the subject
4 creates a feeling of uncertainty in the viewer
5 expresses the change from the old to the new
6 links human figures to the urban landscape
7 was made of objects thrown away by people
8 supports the freedom to read and write
9 disappears from view twice a day
10 is about people who worked in harsh conditions

4 Find words in the text with these meanings.
The paragraph numbers are in brackets.

1 using imagination and skill to make new things (1)
2 a work of art made from stone, metal, wood, etc (2)
3 a number too high to count (3)
4 a work of art that uses objects plus light, sound, etc (3)
5 buildings where works of art are shown to the public (4)
6 containers used to create objects of a certain shape (5)
7 made to go under the surface (5)
8 shown what was hidden (5)
9 the same kind of thing as (6)
10 something that shows you respect someone (8)

6 **Event Horizon** has 31 life-sized bronze male figures standing on top of various buildings in cities such as London, Rotterdam, New York, São Paulo and, in 2015, Hong Kong. The work reflects the fact that nowadays such a high proportion of the world's population lives in cities, with the result that many of us spend all our time in completely man-made environments. The buildings are the modern equivalent of the hills and mountains we used to stand on to view the natural landscape. Gormley's aim in this work, he says, is to make people feel slightly uncomfortable, unsure about what's happening around them. ☐

7 **Waste Man** was a 20-metre-high figure made from 30 tonnes of typical waste material from today's consumer society, including tables, chairs, doors, keyboards, paintings and toilet seats. It was burnt to the ground by the artist during a festival, an event featured in the film **The Margate Exodus**. ☐

8 In 2011 Gormley created **Witness**, an empty iron chair that will stand permanently at the entrance to the British Library in London. The chair is a lifesize version of the symbol used by the authors' charity PEN to represent writers who cannot attend its annual conference because they have been threatened, imprisoned or murdered. It is also a tribute to those who are not free to go to libraries in their own countries. Antony Gormley was knighted in 2014. ☐

1 How important is the theatre in the cultural life of your country? What is your favourite play, and why? Do you ever go to the theatre? Why? / Why not?

2 Look at the picture of Shakespeare's Globe Theatre and the title of the text. What do you think the title means?

Which of these statements about theatre in Shakespeare's time do you think are true? Quickly read the text and check your answers.

1 There were lots of special effects.
2 Music was played during the performances.
3 It was very popular with young people.
4 Everyone in the audience had to stand.
5 The audience were quiet during the performance.
6 The actors didn't learn their lines before the performance.
7 Female characters were played by male actors.

All the World's a Stage

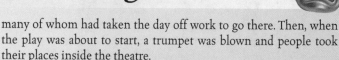

William Shakespeare (1564–1616) is widely considered to be the world's greatest playwright. During his life he wrote at least 38 plays, 154 sonnets and many poems. His plays have been translated into every major language and to this day are performed all over the world.

Shakespeare grew up in the town of Stratford-upon-Avon, but by 1592 his plays were being performed on London stages and he went to live in the capital around that time. There were already several open-air theatres in the city, but the Lord Chamberlain's Men – a theatre company which included Shakespeare – decided that London needed a much grander theatre, and so the Globe was built on the South Bank of the Thames, in 1599.

On the Globe's flag, flown from the top of the theatre, there was a figure of Hercules carrying a globe on his shoulders, together with the motto 'Totus mundus agit histrionem' (the whole world is a playhouse). Shakespeare made this 'all the world's a stage' in his play As You Like It, which was performed at the Globe. Sometimes they flew a flag with a picture of the next play that was on. They also used different colours depending on the type of play: red for a historical drama, white for a comedy and black for a tragedy.

With room for audiences of up to 3,000 people, the Globe was a three-storey amphitheatre that had quite advanced facilities for stage productions. Props and special effects included the use of real cannons, fireworks and smoke for battle scenes, trap-doors in the floor of the stage for surprise entrances by actors, and ropes to enable them to make 'flying' entrances from above. There was also music during performances.

Going to the Globe was fun. There was a holiday atmosphere outside the theatre, with crowds of people – not only theatre-goers – buying goods and refreshments from the market stalls around the building. It was a particularly popular place with young people, many of whom had taken the day off work to go there. Then, when the play was about to start, a trumpet was blown and people took their places inside the theatre.

The cheapest area was called The Pit, where 'commoners' would pay one penny to stand during the production. They would often contribute to the atmosphere of the play, for example by screaming with fright when a 'ghost' appeared. The galleries were occupied by richer individuals, and nobles had seats on the side of the stage itself. Both men and women attended performances, although wealthier women often wore masks to hide their identity.

The actors did not prepare their parts. Instead, a person backstage whispered the lines to the actor just before he was going to say them (female characters were played by young boys, as acting was not viewed as a 'respectable' profession for a woman). Sometimes a complete scene was not explained to the actor until he was actually performing in it, although it is believed that Shakespeare acted in a number of his own plays there.

There was a lot of rivalry between playhouses. Theatres stole plays by sending someone to a performance to copy down all the lines! These stolen plays were called 'Quarto' texts, which meant that alternative, inferior versions of Shakespeare's plays were produced. There was no law of copyright in those days.

In 1613, the original Globe Theatre burnt down when a cannon set fire to its roof during a performance of Shakespeare's Henry VIII. The Globe was rebuilt, but in 1642 the Puritans closed it down, together with all other places of entertainment. In 1644, it was demolished.

A replica of the original, called Shakespeare's Globe Theatre, opened in London in 1997. The first performance in the new theatre was Shakespeare's Henry V. There are also Globe replicas in Italy, the US, and Japan, and an ice replica of the theatre was built in Sweden!

3 Read the text and answer the questions.

1 Why did Shakespeare move to London?
2 What was the reason for building the Globe Theatre?
3 How did the Globe advertise its plays?
4 What did flying a white flag mean?
5 How could actors come onto the stage from below?
6 What kind of people went to the area around the Globe?
7 Why did some women at the Globe cover their faces?
8 How did the actors know what to say on stage?
9 What was a Quarto text?
10 Why was the rebuilt Globe Theatre closed down?

4 Match these words with their meanings a–l.

1	sonnet	7	props	
2	stage	8	part	
3	audience	9	backstage	
4	production	10	lines	
5	comedy	11	scene	
6	tragedy	12	demolished	

a people watching a play, film, etc
b a play that has a sad ending
c a poem with 14 lines that rhyme
d a role in a play
e part of a play in which events happen in one place
f the place in a theatre where actors wait to perform
g a play that is made for the public
h the words spoken by an actor in a play
i a light-hearted play that has a happy ending
j the place in a theatre where actors perform
k destroyed; knocked down
l objects used in a play

What do you think?

- Look at each of the Shakespeare quotes.
- What do they mean?
- Are they still relevant to us today?

1 'The course of true love never did run smooth'

(*A Midsummer Night's Dream*, Act i, Scene 1)

2 ''Tis better to be brief than tedious'

(*Richard III*, Act i, Scene 4)

3 'Better three hours too soon than a minute too late'

(*The Merry Wives of Windsor*, Act ii, Scene 2)

4 'How poor are they that have not patience'

(*Othello*, Act ii, Scene 3)

5 'Kindness, nobler ever than revenge'

(*As You Like It*, Act iv, Scene 3)

6 'If music be the food of love, play on'

(*Twelfth Night*, Act i, Scene 1)

PROJECT

Use the Internet, newspaper articles or magazines to find out more about Shakespeare's Globe Theatre in London.

Write an email to a friend who is visiting London soon. Suggest a visit to the Globe. Write your email in 120–150 words. Include information about:

- where it is and how to get there
- what's on, when, and how much tickets cost
- theatre tours and exhibitions

Education in the UK and US

1 Look at the pictures. Which school do you think is American, and which British? Why? In what ways do you think school life in those countries is different from that in your country?

2 Quickly read the texts. Which paragraphs, in both texts, deal with:

a) school subjects and exams?

b) different types of school?

3 Read both texts. In which country's education system are 1–10 true? Write **UK**, **US**, or **BOTH** next to each.

1 All children must go to school from the age of six.

2 To get into some state secondary schools, children must pass an exam.

3 Only a small minority of children attend private schools.

4 There are boys-only and girls-only schools.

5 At some schools, pupils live at the school.

6 Some children do not go to school.

7 Most state schools make children wear uniforms.

8 In the early years of secondary, all pupils have to study maths.

9 At all schools, pupils are placed in groups according to ability.

10 There are important exams at age 16 and at age 18.

11 The school year consists of two halves.

12 Students who want to go to university are assessed over 4 years.

Education in the United Kingdom

In the United Kingdom it is compulsory to attend school between the ages of five and sixteen, which means that pupils have to go to primary school and then secondary school. Primary education is divided into infant school (age 5–7) and junior school (7–11). At secondary level (11–18), more than 90% of pupils attend state-funded academies or comprehensive schools, which are non-selective and provide education for all children in a particular area. There are about 160 grammar schools in England: to attend these, children have to pass an entrance exam called the 11-plus. About 7% of children are privately educated, in 'public schools' such as Eton, Harrow and Winchester. These usually require the payment of high fees, are often single-sex, and may either be day schools – pupils return home in the evenings – or boarding schools. Uniforms are compulsory in most of these schools, in grammar schools, and in many academies and comprehensive schools. A small minority of children are educated at home.

Schools in the UK, apart from in Scotland, follow the National Curriculum, which means that all schools follow the same syllabus. The school year consists of three terms, and at the end of each year pupils automatically progress to the next level of study, and do not repeat the year, even if they fail the end of year exams. Some schools divide pupils into groups according to ability: this is known as streaming. In the first three years of secondary education, pupils study English, Maths, Science, Design & Technology, Information & Communication Technology (ICT), History, Geography, Modern Foreign Languages, Music, Physical Education, Citizenship and Religious Education. They then choose between eight and ten subjects to study for GCSE (General Certificate of Secondary Education) exams when they are 16. After two years in the sixth form they sit an average of three A-level (Advanced Level) exams, necessary for university entry.

Education in the United States of America

In the US, compulsory education begins at the age of six and then extends, depending on the state, to the age of 16 or 18. Elementary school, sometimes known as grade school, begins with the 1st grade at age 6–7 and continues to the 5th grade at 10–11. Between the ages of 11 and 14, pupils attend junior high school, taking them to the 8th grade, and then on to high school, where, in the 12th grade, they take their high school diploma. High schools can be extremely large, with up to 3,500 pupils. The majority of US students go to state schools: only about 10% attend fee-paying private schools, including boarding schools, and almost 3% are educated at home. There are some single-sex schools, and certain schools require pupils to wear uniforms.

Both state and private schools teach the same core subjects: English, Mathematics, Science, Social Studies and Physical Education, in addition to 'electives' such as Visual Arts, Drama, Technology, Computer Science, Ecology, Creative Writing and Foreign Languages. Pupils are mainstreamed, which means they go to the same school but attend different courses and levels of class. They are graded from A (excellent) to F (failure) in each course on the basis of their performance in tests, class participation, and completion of both written and oral assignments. The school year is divided into two semesters, and twice a year pupils receive a report card with their grades.

To go on to university, called 'college' in America, students must take the SAT (Scholastic Aptitude Test). This is a multiple-choice test that takes about four hours and consists of verbal and mathematical parts. Also taken into account is pupils' GPA (Grade Point Average), the average score taken from all the grades in their final four years of high school. Colleges also test candidates' writing skills by setting them an essay on a given topic.

4 These expressions are explained in the texts. Write down what the text says about each.

1 comprehensive schools
2 grammar schools
3 public schools
4 day schools
5 the National Curriculum
6 streaming
7 GCSE
8 A-level
9 electives
10 mainstreamed
11 SAT
12 GPA

5 Match these words from the texts with meanings a–l.

1	compulsory	7	sixth form
2	entrance exam	8	sit
3	fees	9	core
4	boarding	10	assignments
5	uniforms	11	semesters
6	terms	12	candidates

a money paid for a professional service
b take (an exam)
c something you have to do
d set of clothes worn by pupils
e two periods of time that the school year is divided into
f three periods of time that the school year is divided into
g the most important (school subjects)
h (school) where pupils live all the time
i people taking an exam or wanting a place at college, a job, etc
j pieces of work that people are given to do
k test enabling people to get into a school, college, etc
l final two years of secondary school for pupils aged 16–18

What do you think?

In which country, the UK or US, would you prefer to study? Why? Are the following good ideas? Why? / Why not?

- single-sex schools
- selection and streaming
- being educated at home
- repeating school years if exam results are poor
- private education for people whose parents can afford it
- school uniforms
- boarding schools
- being able to choose from a wide range of school subjects

PROJECT

Draw a table comparing the school systems in the UK, US and your country. Include information about ages, types of school, subjects, exams, terms and university entrance.

LITERATURE

Jane Austen – *Pride and Prejudice*

1 Why do people in your country get married? In the past, what other reasons were there for getting married?

2 Read this description of the novel *Pride and Prejudice* and complete the notes.

Pride and Prejudice, by __Jane Austen__

Year of publication: ¹_____

Type of novel: ²_____

Context: the English ³_____ system

Theme: love and ⁴_____

Setting: ⁵_____, in England

Main characters:

• Mrs ⁶_____

• her ⁷_____ daughters

• Mr Wickham, who has a relationship with ⁸_____

• Mr ⁹_____, a rich neighbour, who marries ¹⁰_____

• Mr ¹¹_____, his friend, who marries ¹²_____

Pride and Prejudice

PRIDE AND PREJUDICE by Jane Austen was published in 1813. Like all of her novels, *Pride and Prejudice* is a comedy of manners which describes in detail the customs, behaviours and habits of people. In 19th century England there was a class system which parallels the social class system of today. Women usually married men of the same class. For the upper classes, marriage was much more like a business transaction than it is today. Even among poor families, marriage contracts could include financial conditions and a dowry. Marriage was the only way of social improvement for a woman.

The novel tells the story of the Bennet family in Hertfordshire, who try to overcome social barriers that separate them from their aristocratic neighbours. Mrs Bennet wants to find husbands for her five daughters, Jane, Elizabeth, Lydia, Kitty and Mary, because when her husband dies his estate will go to the cousin Mr Collins and so her daughters will inherit nothing. She is very happy when Charles Bingley, a rich young bachelor, moves to live near them with his two sisters and rich friend Mr Darcy. Bingley falls in love with Jane and Darcy is attracted to her sister Elizabeth. At first, Elizabeth does not like Darcy as she thinks he is arrogant. But, when Lydia runs away with Mr Wickham, Mr Darcy convinces them to return and marry to protect the family honour. As time passes, Elizabeth falls in love with Darcy and the novel ends with Elizabeth accepting his proposal of marriage and Jane marrying Bingley.

3 Match these words and phrases with their meanings.

> comedy of manners
> dowry
> social improvement
> social barrier
> business transaction
> aristocratic
> estate
> inherit
> bachelor
> proposal

1 an unmarried man

2 a formal request or offer

3 receive property and money after somebody's death

4 something that keeps people of different classes apart

5 of the highest social class

6 changing a person's situation for the better

7 light-hearted novel about how people behave with each other

8 money given by a woman's family to the man she marries

9 the property and money that somebody leaves when they die

10 the act of buying or selling something to make money

4 Read the opening extract from *Pride and Prejudice*, and answer the questions.

CHAPTER 1

IT IS A TRUTH universally acknowledged, that a single man in possession of a good fortune, must be in want of a wife.

However little known the feelings or views of such a man may be on his first entering a neighbourhood, this truth is so well fixed in the minds of the surrounding families, that he is considered the rightful property of some one or other of their daughters.

'My dear Mr Bennet,' said his lady to him one day, 'have you heard that Netherfield Park is let at last?'

Mr Bennet replied that he had not.

'But it is,' returned she; 'for Mrs Long has just been here, and she told me all about it.'

Mr Bennet made no answer.

'Do you not want to know who has taken it?' cried his wife impatiently.

'You want to tell me, and I have no objection to hearing it.'

This was invitation enough.

'Why, my dear, you must know, Mrs Long says that Netherfield is taken by a young man of large fortune from the north of England; that he came down on Monday in a chaise and four to see the place, and was so much delighted with it, that he agreed with Mr Morris immediately; that he is to take possession before Michaelmas, and some of his servants are to be in the house by the end of next week.'

'What is his name?'

'Bingley.'

'Is he married or single?'

'Oh! Single, my dear, to be sure! A single man of large fortune; four or five thousand a year. What a fine thing for our girls!'

'How so? How can it affect them?'

'My dear Mr Bennet,' replied his wife, 'how can you be so tiresome! You must know that I am thinking of his marrying one of them.'

'Is that his design in settling here?'

'Design! Nonsense, how can you talk so! But it is very likely that he may fall in love with one of them, and therefore you must visit him as soon as he comes.'

1 What does the first sentence mean? What does it suggest about attitudes to marriage two centuries ago?
2 Where do you think this conversation takes place?
3 Why do you think Mrs Bennet addresses her husband as 'My dear Mr Bennet'?
4 'Netherfield Park' is a large house. What do you think 'let' means here?
5 How do Mr and Mrs Bennet differ in their reactions to the news about Netherfield Park? How does the author's use of irony make this extract amusing?

> 'Do you not want to know who has taken it?' cried his wife impatiently.
> 'You want to tell me, and I have no objection to hearing it.'
> This was invitation enough.

6 Given that it is the early 19th century, what form of transport is a 'chaise and four' likely to be?
7 How much does Mr Bingley earn?
8 Why is Mrs Bennet so excited?
9 What do you think 'design' means here?
10 What does Mrs Bennet want her husband to do?

What do you think?

- Can marrying for money or social status lead to happiness?
- Do you think 'arranged marriages' can work? Are parents sometimes better able to choose suitable partners for their sons and daughters?
- How serious a social issue is child marriage around the world? What can be done about it?

PROJECT

Choose a novel, film or play about love and make notes about it similar to those in exercise 2 on page 18. Then write a short review of it in about 150 words.

5

1 In pairs, match the five food items to the number of calories they contain. How many calories, approximately, should you eat in a day?

108	760	44	162	800

2 Discuss these questions with your partner.

1 What is 'fast food', and why is it sometimes called 'junk food'? How often do you eat it? Why?

2 Is all fast food bad? Can you think of any examples of healthy fast food?

3 Apart from eating too much unhealthy food, what else can make people overweight?

4 How can schools help students to live healthier lifestyles?

3 Read the text and write headings **A–F** above paragraphs 1–6.

A Changing mealtimes everywhere

B Why Americans love fast food

C Improving food in British schools

D Americans getting even fatter

E Unhealthy American schools

F The amount that Americans eat

People are getting fatter, faster than ever

1 _____

Over the past 25 years, the adult obesity rate has risen steadily in all 50 American states, and now ranges from 20% in Colorado to 36% in Louisiana. Despite campaigns to make people aware of the dangers of over-eating, about 137 million, or 70.7% of US adults, are either overweight or obese. Worryingly, this figure is predicted to rise even higher. What does this mean for America? Already up to 400,000 deaths each year may be caused by obesity (only smoking kills more people), and the annual cost to the country is currently nearly $120 billion. Cases of diabetes, coronary heart disease, stroke and certain types of cancer are all likely to increase further.

2 _____

Many people blame the fast food industry, along with sedentary lifestyles, for the worrying increase. The average American now consumes about three hamburgers and four portions of French fries every week. That's 90 grams of fat and 2,250 calories (the average person needs about 2,000 calories a day). A recent survey found that more than a third of American children eat fast food every day.

3 _____

Most Americans know that fast food isn't good for them, as it is high in calories, fat, salt and sugar. Yet fast-food restaurants are part of American life. After World War II, higher salaries and productivity, together with technological developments and increased consumerism, made the fast-food restaurant popular. It represented a modern lifestyle, and is still a popular place for teenagers to get together with friends. The food is cheap, and many say they love the taste. The advertising is often aimed at children, with offers of entertainment and free gifts.

4 _____

Another factor in fast-food sales – not only in the US, but all over the world – is our increasingly busy lifestyles. In the past, families ate a home-cooked meal together at dinner time. These days, meals can be eaten at any hour of the day, and people rely on easy, instant food – not always nutritious – that is available '24/7'. America invented the 'TV dinner', and it is something most people around the world now enjoy.

5 _____

Finding nutritious food is also difficult in schools, which often have contracts with fast-food suppliers and drinks companies. Exercise in schools has become less important too. A recent report showed that only one in four US children aged 12 to 15 meet the government's recommendations of at least 60 minutes moderate to vigorous daily activity. But obesity is no longer only America's problem – Europe is also getting fatter. It is estimated that 33% of girls and 25% of boys in the UK aged 2–19 are either overweight or obese.

6 _____

Food and nutrition in schools has a direct influence on students' performance in the classroom and poor diet has negative effects on both concentration and behaviour. Jamie Oliver, a British celebrity chef, introduced the idea of healthier school food in a TV programme some years ago. As a result of this, many schools in England changed their lunch menus and introduced vending machines selling fresh fruit, nuts and yogurt drinks. These, however, are not always popular with the pupils, who continue to buy junk food outside school for snacks and lunch. It is important to educate students about diet, nutrition and healthy eating habits, and this needs to happen in schools.

4 Find words in the text with these meanings. The paragraph numbers are in brackets.

1　the condition of being unhealthily overweight (1)
2　not active, sitting down a lot (2)
3　amount of food for one person (2)
4　buying and using lots of goods and services (3)
5　(food that is) very good for your health (4)
6　all day and night, every day of the week (4)
7　using a lot of strength or energy (5)
8　agreements made in writing (5)
9　the food that a person usually eats (6)
10　that sells things (6)

5 Read the text again carefully. Are these statements True (*T*) or False (*F*)?

1　Smoking causes more deaths in the US than obesity.
2　On average, Americans eat one hamburger a day.
3　Fast food restaurants are a very recent invention.
4　Nowadays, fewer people have meals with their families.
5　The idea of the 'TV dinner' first started in Britain.
6　Many American teenagers do too little exercise.
7　Young people who don't eat well do badly at school.
8　All British students want to eat healthy food at school.

What do you think?

- Is unhealthy eating a problem in your country? Could changing lifestyles make it a problem?
- Do young people get enough exercise? If not, what can be done about it?
- How healthy are the snacks and drinks sold in the vending machines where you study or work?
- Whose responsibility is it to ensure healthy eating in schools? The school, the parents, the government, or the young people themselves? Or all of these? Why?

PROJECT

Note down everything you have eaten in the last three days and put it into the following categories: proteins, dairy, fruit, oils / fats / sugars, vegetables, carbohydrates. Then write a brief diary entry with some ideas for improving your diet.

LITERATURE

Percy Shelley – *Ozymandias*

1 Complete the text about Percy Shelley using the words in the box.

chapters   masterpieces   pamphlet   poetry   prose   Romantic   stanzas

PERCY BYSSHE SHELLEY (1792–1822) was born in Field Place, the family home in Sussex, and educated at the **exclusive** Eton College, where he was frequently bullied. His father was a Member of Parliament. In 1810 he entered University College Oxford, where he often preferred to read books of his own choice rather than attend lectures, and was **expelled** in 1811 after publishing a ¹_____ entitled The Necessity of Atheism.

He then **eloped** with 16-year-old Harriet Westbrook and for the next three years engaged in radical politics and lived in various parts of Britain. His marriage to Harriet caused a serious **rift** with his family, particularly his father, who refused all contact with Percy and ended his **allowance**. Partly as a consequence of this he would always have financial difficulties, as even his finest ²_____ was not widely read during his lifetime.

In 1813 Percy privately distributed his first major poem, *Queen Mab*, in which he expressed many of his strongest feelings, including his commitment to vegetarianism and his indignation about **tyranny** in the world. Before long Shelley, together with John Keats and Lord Byron, was to become one of the most notable of the 19th century British ³_____ Poets, who placed great importance on freedom, imagination, idealism, emotions and passions, as well as a love of both nature and the supernatural.

In 1814 he met and eloped with Mary Godwin, daughter of the feminist author Mary Wollstonecraft and the left-wing philosopher William Godwin. They married shortly after Harriet's suicide in 1816, and in that year Mary began writing the first ⁴_____ of her famous novel *Frankenstein*, which was published two years later.

In 1816 Shelley and Mary spent time with Byron in Geneva and visited the Alps, a visit which **inspired** Shelley's poem *Mont Blanc*. In 1818 Shelley published his longest poem, *The Revolt of Islam*, consisting of over 500 nine-line ⁵_____. Later that year he and Mary left England **for good** and moved to Italy, living in various cities and towns including Rome, Florence and Pisa, and spending more time with Byron. In Italy Shelley wrote a series of ⁶_____ including *Prometheus Unbound*, *Julian and Maddalo*, *Epipsychidion* and *Adonais*; shorter poems such as *To a Skylark* and *Ode to the West Wind*; and his greatest ⁷_____ work, the essay *A Defence of Poetry*.

Tragically, Percy Shelley **drowned** off the Italian coast shortly before his 30th birthday while sailing from Livorno to Lerici. His body was cremated and his ashes buried in the Protestant Cemetery, Rome. Despite his fiercely **anti-establishment** beliefs, Shelley was eventually given a memorial in Poet's Corner at Westminster Abbey.

2 Read the text to check your answers.

3 Match the bold words in the text with definitions a–j.

a forever
b ran away secretly to get married
c died in the water because it was impossible to breathe
d the cruel and unfair use of power
e money given regularly
f disagreement that harms a relationship
g forced to leave
h against the people in power in a country
i expensive and only for rich or upper-class people
j gave someone the idea of creating something

4 Answer the questions about the text.

1 What happened to Shelley at school?
2 Why do you think he had to leave university?
3 Why did he have money problems as an adult?
4 In what ways did *Queen Mab* reflect the values of the Romantic Poets?
5 What is Mary Shelley best known for nowadays?
6 In which country did Percy write many of his best works?
7 How did he die and at what age?
8 Where is Shelley's grave?

5 Read Shelley's poem *Ozymandias*. Then answer the questions.

1 What is the theme of the poem?
2 There are 14 lines in the poem. How many lines does the first part have? How many are there in the second part? What kind of poem always has this form?
3 What is the rhyme scheme of this poem? Which words form half-rhymes, e.g. 'stone' with 'frown'?

Ozymandias

ॐ

I met a traveller from an antique land
Who said: "Two vast and trunkless legs of stone
Stand in the desert. Near them, on the sand,
Half sunk, a shattered visage lies, whose frown,
And wrinkled lip, and sneer of cold command,
Tell that its sculptor well those passions read
Which yet survive, stamped on these lifeless things,
The hand that mocked them and the heart that fed:
And on the pedestal these words appear:
'My name is Ozymandias, king of kings:
Look on my works, ye Mighty, and despair!'
Nothing beside remains. Round the decay
Of that colossal wreck, boundless and bare
The lone and level sands stretch far away."

6 Read the poem again and answer the questions.

1 Has the poet actually seen the sculpture of Ozymandias? Which words tell you?
2 What does the face of the statue tell us about the king's character?
3 What does the writing on the pedestal tell us about him?
4 Explain the irony in the line 'Look on my works, ye Mighty, and despair!'
5 What do we learn about the sculptor?
6 What does *Ozymandias* say about the nature of power and powerful individuals?
7 What does the poem say about the nature of art?
8 What does the last line seem to be saying about powerful people after they die?

7 Choose the correct meaning of these words from the poem.

1 **antique**	a modern	b very old
2 **shattered**	a broken	b handsome
3 **visage**	a face	b message
4 **frown**	a smile	b annoyed look
5 **wrinkled**	a with small lines	b smooth
6 **sneer**	a look of respect	b look of no respect
7 **mocked**	a made fun of	b admired
8 **mighty**	a ordinary people	b powerful people
9 **despair**	a feel happy	b lose all hope
10 **decay**	a slow destruction	b rebuilding
11 **wreck**	a wonderful object	b ruined object
12 **boundless**	a without end	b beautiful

8 Find examples of the following in the poem.

1 *Assonance* – the repeated use of the same vowel sound in stressed syllables that are close to each other.
2 *Alliteration* – the repeated use of the same letter and sound, especially at the beginning of words.
3 *Sibilance* – the repetition of soft consonant sounds, especially /s/ or /ʃ/ to give a hissing effect.

What do you think?

- Is it ever possible for one person to use great power wisely and fairly? Why? / Why not?
- Which present-day leaders should read this poem? Why?
- How would you like people to remember you in the future?

PROJECT

Think of someone from history who had complete power over their country. Write a brief FactFile about that person, including how they used that power, how they treated their people and how he or she is remembered today. Use the Internet and/or books to help you.

London West End Theatre

1 Which cities in the world are particularly famous for their theatres?
Which of the plays and shows in the pictures would you like to see? Why?

2 The text has seven paragraphs. Read the text. Which paragraphs belong to these four sections?

| What the West End is | The history of the West End | The early history of the West End | The West End today |

LONDON'S THEATRELAND

1 The West End is the largest theatre district in the world and is the centre of British commercial theatre. The West End originally took its name from the fact that it was situated to the West of the City of London. Theatreland, the heart of the West End, is bordered by The Strand to the south, Oxford Street to the north, Regent Street to the west and Kingsway to the east.

2 London's first playhouse was built at Shoreditch in 1576 and had the wholly appropriate name of The Theatre. Prior to this, plays had been performed in ad hoc venues such as courtyards, inn-yards or spacious private homes. When the lease on The Theatre ran out in 1597, its owner, Richard Burbage, transported its timber across the Thames and used it to build the first Globe Theatre on the South Bank, which opened in 1599.

3 The first West End venue opened in 1663 when the first of several theatres was opened on Drury Lane. This venue played host to the earliest West End stars such as Nell Gwyn and Charles Hart, until it was destroyed by fire in 1672. A new theatre, called the Theatre Royal, in Drury Lane, was designed by Christopher Wren (the architect of St Paul's Cathedral) and opened on the same site in 1674. This second theatre survived for the next 120 years, during which time several other theatres, such as the Haymarket and the Theatre Royal Covent Garden (now the Royal Opera House) were built and the notion of West End theatre evolved.

4 Today's West End began taking shape in the 19th Century, when many of the imposing and beautiful theatre buildings still standing today were erected, and theatre-going became highly fashionable among the middle and upper classes. The backbone of the West End was finally put in place towards the end of the century, when Shaftesbury Avenue was created, and theatres were soon built along it.

5 New West End theatres continued to be built throughout the early years of the 20th century, while the post-war years saw the opening of London's two great, modern, centres of

theatre: The National Theatre and the Barbican. Although the rise of alternative entertainments such as the cinema, and the cost of maintaining such extravagant buildings, posed a constant challenge, West End theatre has continued to thrive in the modern era.

6 Total annual West End attendances rose to 14.7 million in 2014, giving it the largest theatre audience of any English-speaking country. That's more than attend all of England's Premier League football matches in a year. One of the reasons for the recent increase in ticket sales has been the staging of hit musicals such as *The Lion King*, *Thriller Live*, *Wicked*, *We Will Rock You* and *Jersey Boys*. Another is the appearance of well-known screen actors like Daniel Radcliffe (of *Harry Potter* fame) in *Rosencrantz and Guildenstern are Dead*, David Tennant (*Doctor Who*) in *Don Juan in Soho*, Patrick Stewart (*Star Trek*) in *No Man's Land* and Damian Lewis (*Homeland*) in *The Goat, Or Who is Sylvia?* American actors on the West End stage include Ed Harris (*Westworld*) in *Buried Child*, Amber Riley (*Glee*) in *Dreamgirls* and Michael C Hall (*Dexter*) in *Lazarus*.

7 The Society of London Theatre (SOLT) produces the London Theatre Guide, the definitive guide to what's on in London theatre, and hosts officiallondontheatre.co.uk, which is recognized as one of the UK's leading arts websites. SOLT also organizes the Laurence Olivier Awards, London theatre's most prestigious awards, and organizes Kids Week, an annual promotion aimed at introducing young people to the world of theatre.

3 Read the text again. When did each of the following happen?

1 the building of the first theatre in London
2 the opening of the Globe Theatre
3 the opening of the first Drury Lane Theatre
4 the burning down of the first Drury Lane Theatre
5 the opening of the Theatre Royal in Drury Lane
6 the West End, as we know it now, started to develop
7 large numbers of richer people started going to the theatre
8 the creation of Shaftesbury Avenue

4 Find expressions with these meanings. The paragraph numbers are in brackets.

1 arranged spontaneously (2)
2 places where people go for an event (2)
3 rental agreement for a property (2)
4 was the place where people were invited to perform (3)
5 the most important part of (4)
6 costing more money than necessary (5)
7 be very successful and profitable (5)
8 the number of people at performances (6)

5 Answer the questions about the text.

1 What is the origin of the name 'West End'? What is 'Theatreland'?
2 Before 1576, where did people watch plays?
3 What was the wood from The Theatre used for?
4 On which street were many theatres built in the 19th century?
5 What difficulties did the theatres face in the 20th century?
6 Why are more people going to West End theatres?
7 Where can more information on West End theatres be obtained?
8 What does SOLT do for young people every year?

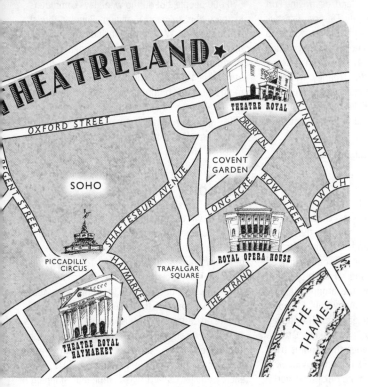

What do you think?

- Have you seen a hit musical on stage? In what ways are musicals and plays performed in the theatre different from film versions? Which do you prefer? Why?
- Would you go to the theatre specially to see a famous actor on stage? Why? / Why not?
- Are enough theatre productions aimed at people of school age, and those over 65? Should theatre tickets be much cheaper for people of school age?
- Have you ever acted on stage? If so, what did you enjoy about it? If not, would you like to? Why / Why not?

PROJECT

Choose a West End musical and produce a leaflet to advertise it. Use the Internet, magazines and newspapers to find out more about it. Think about:

- what the musical is about
- the music
- the cast
- why audiences enjoy it
- special offers for tickets

1 What is special about the capital city of your country? What would you advise visitors to see and do there?

2 Read these six short texts. Put the cities in order according to the size of their permanent populations: from largest ☐1 to smallest ☐6 .

Canberra

Kingston

Ottawa

Canberra ☐

Most people think that the capital of Australia is Sydney. In fact, a century ago, there was so much rivalry between Australia's two biggest cities, Melbourne and Sydney, that a completely new city was created to be the nation's capital. That city, located at a roughly equal distance from the two rivals, is Canberra and it is one of only two completely planned capitals in the world. Today it has 380,000 inhabitants, and among its unusual features is an artificial lake – Lake Burley Griffin – right in the city centre, and the tranquil National Botanic Gardens, with a marvellous collection of Australia's weird and wonderful trees and plants.

Kingston ☐

The Caribbean island of Jamaica was discovered by Columbus in 1494 and remained a Spanish colony until the English seized it in 1655. The capital, Kingston, was founded in 1693, when a massive earthquake hit the island, destroying Port Royal, until then the main city. Despite disasters such as hurricanes and earthquakes, Kingston has continued to grow and now has a population of about one million, mostly of African descent. Attractions include the Bob Marley Museum, dedicated to the great Jamaican reggae musician, and the University of the West Indies, founded in 1962, the year of the country's independence from Britain.

Ottawa ☐

Ottawa, located between the much bigger cities of Montreal and Toronto, was chosen as the capital of Canada in 1857. Lying on the border between Canada East and Canada West, it seemed the ideal compromise in a country divided into English-speaking and French-speaking communities. Today, Ottawa has around 900,000 inhabitants and houses many of Canada's national museums and art galleries. The Rideau Canal passes through the city, linking Ottawa with Lake Ontario. In summer, the canal is used for boating, swimming and fishing; in winter, it becomes the longest ice-skating rink in the world.

Pretoria ☐

South Africa has three capital cities. Cape Town is the legislative capital, Bloemfontein is the judicial capital, and Pretoria – or Tshwane – is the administrative capital. It was founded in 1855 by Marthinus Pretorius, a descendant of Dutch settlers, and today has a population of 750,000 people. Jacaranda trees with purple flowers line its streets and some people call it Jacaranda City. One of its most famous places is Church Square. Here, in 1963 during the Rivonia Trial at the Palace of Justice, Nelson Mandela was charged with treason and imprisoned. Church Square is off Church Street, which is one of the longest straight streets in the world.

Washington DC ☐

Washington DC (the 'DC' stands for *District of Columbia*) is the capital of the United States of America. It has an official population of about 670,000 people, but during weekdays commuters increase this to over 1 million. Popular tourist destinations in Washington include the Capitol, the Jefferson Memorial, and the residence of the President of the United States: the White House, at number 1600 Pennsylvania Avenue. It has 132 rooms and 35 bathrooms. President Theodore Roosevelt gave the White House its name in 1901, although it was first painted white during rebuilding after it had been set on fire by the British in 1814.

London ☐

London, with a population of approximately 8.7 million people, is the capital of the United Kingdom. It has a changing skyline with many new skyscrapers, including the 180-metre tall Swiss Re-insurance tower in the City, nicknamed 'the Gherkin' because of its unique shape. Another landmark is the 235-metre One Canada Square on Canary Wharf. It is known to Londoners as 'the vertical Fleet Street', as many national newspapers have moved there from their traditional offices in Fleet Street. In 2012, the energy-efficient Shard was completed. Standing at over 300 metres, it was designed to resemble the church spires of historic London.

Pretoria

Washington DC

'The Gherkin', London

The Shard, London

3 Work in pairs, Student **A** and Student **B**.

> Student **A**: Read about Canberra, Ottawa and London
> Student **B**: Read about Kingston, Pretoria and Washington

While you read, underline one historical fact and one fact about the modern-day city. When you finish reading, tell your partner about them.

4 Read the texts again and complete the table with information about all six capitals.

City	Country	Places to visit
Canberra		
Kingston		
Ottawa		
Pretoria		
Washington		
London		

5 Match the words from each text with meanings 1–12 below.

> **Canberra:** artificial   **Kingston:** founded / descent / dedicated to
> **Ottawa:** located   **Pretoria:** legislative / judicial / administrative
> **Washington:** commuters   **London:** skyline / landmark / nicknamed

1 the shape made by a number of tall buildings
2 describing the exact place where something is
3 started (as a city, organization, etc)
4 in memory of
5 given an informal name by people
6 not natural
7 connected with running a country, company, etc
8 family origins
9 building that can be seen clearly from a distance
10 connected with courts and judges
11 people who travel into the city to work every day
12 connected with making new laws

What do you think?

- Which of these capital cities would you like to visit, and which not? Why? Which other cities would you like to visit? What would you like to do there?

PROJECT

Do some research on your own capital city, then write an email to an English-speaking friend, inviting them to visit it. Include information on:
- where the city is, its population and a little about its history
- what its famous landmarks are
- what they could do there and which places they could visit

1 What do you know about Australia? Complete the paragraph with these words and numbers.

| harbour | 19 | coral | 7.6 | outback | 32 |
| marsupials | 2,600 | monolith | 348 |

With a land mass of roughly [1]_____ million km[2], Australia is [2]_____ times larger than the United Kingdom, but with a population of only about [3]_____ million people. Australia is famous for its landmarks of natural beauty, such as the Great Barrier Reef, which at [4]_____ km[2] is the world's biggest [5]_____ reef – and also the largest living organism on Earth. The hot, dry interior of the country is known as the [6]_____ , and right in the middle is Ayer's Rock, or Uluru, the world's biggest [7]_____ . This huge red rock stands [8]_____ metres in height, and is a sacred site for the aboriginal people. Australia is also known for its unusual animals, including [9]_____ such as kangaroos, which carry their young in pouches. Sydney, the biggest city, has the world's largest natural [10]_____ , crossed by the famous bridge facing its unique opera house.

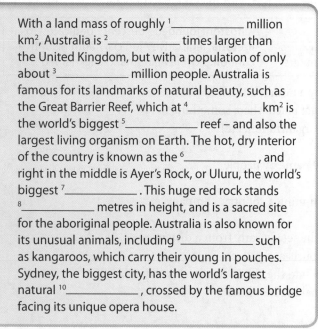

2 For over 200 years, people have emigrated to Australia. Which of 1–6, do you think, are reasons why many people went to live there?

1 to become sheep farmers
2 to fish in the seas
3 to find gold
4 to find jobs
5 to convert people to their religion
6 to serve prison sentences

Now read the text quickly to check your answers.

Immigration to Australia

The word 'aboriginal' means 'from the beginning', and the Aborigines were indeed the original inhabitants of Australia. They themselves were once immigrants, originally from Africa, and first settled in Australia over 42,000 years ago.

The first ship to land Europeans on Australian soil, the Eendracht, was Dutch, and arrived there in 1616. In 1642 another Dutch explorer, Abel Tasman, discovered the island we now call Tasmania. However, the Dutch did not think that the land they called 'New Holland' was worth formally occupying, and it wasn't until 1770 that it was officially claimed for Britain by Captain James Cook. Britain formally colonized the area in 1786, calling it New South Wales. The British were mainly interested in this seemingly inhospitable land because it was an ideal place to start a new prison settlement. Britain was suffering from overcrowded prisons at home, having lost their prison colonies in the United States after the War of Independence.

In 1788, the first fleet of 11 ships and 1,350 people (the majority of them convicts) arrived in Australia at Sydney Cove. From about 1815 the colony began to grow. Although the journey from Europe took over a year and was very difficult, people began to hear that Australia wasn't just a prison colony, but also a fine place for anyone to make a fresh start in life, and that some people were making a fortune there from the free land they could use for sheep farming. In 1850 the discovery of gold attracted many more Europeans – two per cent of the population of Britain and Ireland moved to Australia during the following Gold Rush.

Inevitably there was increased conflict with the Aborigines, who were brutally hunted and poisoned by the settlers. Aboriginal children were taken away from their parents to be educated by white people. Australians had also been alarmed by the numbers of Chinese immigrants during the Gold Rush, and the White Australia Policy was established in 1901 to restrict non-white settlers. Any new immigrant

3 Read the text and answer the questions.

1 Who were the first people to live in Australia? Where did they come from?
2 What did early Dutch explorers think of Australia?
3 Why did the British decide to colonize it?
4 What factors attracted settlers in the 19th century?
5 How did the settlers treat the aboriginal people?
6 Why did Australia bring in language tests for immigrants?
7 How did Australia encourage European immigration after World War II?
8 Where have more immigrants come from recently? Why?

The Immigrants' Ship 1884, by John Charles Dollman

had to pass a dictation test in a European language chosen by the immigration officer, and if the immigrants were seen as unwelcome, it was easy to choose a language they didn't know. The most famous case was in 1934, when Egon Kisch, a left-wing Czechoslovakian journalist, tried to enter Australia. He could speak five languages, but failed a test in Scottish Gaelic, and was deported as illiterate!

After World War II, as its economy expanded, Australia established a huge immigration programme. More than two million Europeans emigrated to Australia between 1945 and 1965 to escape post-war poverty and unemployment. Most of them came from Britain and Ireland, but there were also large numbers arriving from the Netherlands, Germany, Greece, Italy, Yugoslavia, and Turkey. The Australian government helped many of them financially by paying for their journey and giving them somewhere to live until they found a job. The White Australia Policy ended in 1973, and this greatly changed the character of Australian society, which became much less conservative and monocultural. Later waves of immigration have brought the total number of settlers since 1945 to nearly 7 million, with a recent increase in those arriving from Asia.

4 Match these words from the text with their meanings a–l.

1	soil		7	fortune	
2	claimed		8	conflict	
3	inhospitable		9	brutally	
4	settlement		10	deported	
5	overcrowded		11	policy	
6	convicts		12	monocultural	

a with too many people inside
b consisting of people of only one race, language or religion
c land
d forced to leave a country, by law
e a place where people have come to live
f people who have been found guilty of a crime
g said to belong to you
h plan of action chosen by a government or company
i a very large amount of money
j unpleasant to live in
k fighting
l with great violence and cruelty

What do you think?

- What do you think are the factors, apart from work, that attract people to Australia nowadays?
- Would you like to live there? Why? / Why not?
- How should people treat the original inhabitants of countries they settle in?

PROJECT

In groups, imagine you have established a new country on an island. What would your immigration policies be? Think about the following options and write a speech explaining your country's immigration policy. Give your speeches to the class and see which policy gets the most votes.

1 only allow in people who have skills that are needed on the island
2 only allow in people from your country of birth, or who speak your language
3 allow in certain numbers of people of different ages, professions, salaries, etc
4 allow in anybody who was unemployed or living in poverty in their own country
5 only allow in people who have artistic or other creative talents
6 allow in anybody who wants to live on the island

9A

1 What's happening in the picture? Would you see similar scenes on the streets in your country?

2 Read the text. What is the writer's main aim?

A to criticize British children for their bad behaviour

B to describe the problems faced by British children

C to suggest ways of improving British children's lives

D to compare today's children with previous generations

Britain's unhappy and unhealthy children

British children are among the unhappiest and unhealthiest in Europe, according to a new league table. Research comparing children's **well-being** across 25 countries paints a picture of **dysfunctional** British families failing to talk to each other or eat together.

Youngsters in Britain are most likely to come from **broken homes** and have among the poorest relationships with their parents and friends. Young Britons also have some of the worst eating habits and freely admit **binge-drinking** and other self-destructive activities.

The study by the University of York (see map inside front cover) ranked British youngsters 21st out of the 25 EU countries surveyed on a scale of 'child well-being'. Children were worse off only in Latvia, Estonia, Lithuania and Slovakia. The findings have caused renewed concern over the effects of divorce and family breakdown and resulted in demands for ministers to do more to prevent the breakdown of the traditional family.

The study found that British youngsters were most likely to live in family set-ups linked with reduced success at school and beyond. 'There is substantial evidence that children in single-parent families as well as in **step-families** tend to have worse outcomes than **peers** living with both biological parents, it said.

The researchers actually found that many children in Britain are **barely** on speaking terms with their parents. Just 60 per cent spoke to their parents several times a week while only 67 per cent sat at the table to eat with their parents – the lowest proportion in Europe.

Many were unhappy at school and felt 'pressured', while fewer than 50% of youngsters aged between 11 and 15 regarded their friends as 'kind and helpful'. Meanwhile, British children were among the fattest and the least likely to eat fruit or have breakfast, with 33% now classed as too big, one of the highest figures in Europe. British children were also more likely than peers in any other nation to resort to 'risky behaviour': more than 25% of 15-year-olds had been drunk 20 times or more, the second highest in Europe.

Youngsters in Britain also have greater experience of **bullying** and fighting at school than peers in most other nations. Research for Childline, Britain's telephone advice service for children who feel in danger, found that 51% of children in primary schools and 54% in secondary schools saw bullying as a real problem in their school. And a recent survey of 7,000 teenagers found that nearly 60% had been bullied in some way, including 13% who had been 'severely bullied'.

There is also the growing problem of cyberbullying – the use of the Internet, mobile phones or other technologies to threaten or embarrass others. Many young people are subjected to upsetting 'hate mails' and messages via email, chatrooms and mobile phone texting, and these forms of communication are sometimes used to encourage others to take part in the bullying. Bullies also access personal information and photos on social networking sites like Instagram and Facebook and use it to make fun of their victims, often by placing it on other sites without their permission. Possibly most alarming of all is cyber-blackmail, which may involve obtaining embarrassing photos of someone, often by tricking him or her, and then threatening to share the pictures by mobile phone or the Internet with friends, family or the public, unless money is paid.

Professor Jonathan Bradshaw, co-author of the York study, said: 'It paints a very sad picture of children in Britain. They are **marginalized** by society and treated like second-class citizens.' It is clear that rising **affluence** has done nothing to improve British children's lives, and that toys, technology and other material possessions do not necessarily bring happiness.

3 Match the bold words in the text with these meanings.

1 general health and happiness
2 not working properly
3 backgrounds where the parents have separated
4 consuming a lot of alcohol in a short time
5 families formed by marriage to someone who already has children
6 people of the same age as someone
7 almost not at all
8 deliberately hurting or scaring a weaker person
9 made to feel that they are not important
10 having lots of money

4 Complete the notes about British children with figures from the text.

- Child well-being – position of UK children: ^{1}_____ out of 25.
- Percentage having meals with parents: ^{2}_____
- Percentage with positive opinion of friends: under ^{3}_____
- Percentage overweight: ^{4}_____
- Percentage of 15-year-olds repeatedly drunk: over ^{5}_____
- Percentage of secondary school pupils concerned about bullying: ^{6}_____
- Percentage of young people victims of bullying: ^{7}_____
- Percentage of young people victims of severe bullying: ^{8}_____

5 Answer the questions about the text.

1 Following the results of the study, what do some people want the government to do?
2 Which children, according to the study, are generally less successful?
3 In what way do many UK children have a poor relationship with their parents?
4 What do you think 'pressured' (paragraph 6) means?
5 What is 'Childline' (paragraph 7)?
6 What examples of bad eating habits are given?
7 How do cyberbullies contact their victims? What do they get other bullies to do?
8 How do bullies use social networking sites? What do they want to do?
9 How, according to Professor Bradshaw, are children treated by British society?

What do you think?

- Are you surprised that 'material possessions do not bring happiness' to young people? Why? / Why not?
- Where do you think your country would be on the scale of child well-being mentioned in the text? What are the advantages and disadvantages of being a young person where you live? Do the disadvantages include any of the dangers and difficulties faced by British children? Why? / Why not?
- Do you think studies like this give an unfairly negative impression of young people today?

PROJECT

Use the Internet, newspapers and magazines to find out more about the problem of cyberbullying among young people in your country, and write an article about it. Think about:

- how widespread the problem is
- whether the situation of cyberbullying is improving or getting worse
- the effects of it
- the reasons for it
- possible solutions to it

1 What are your happiest memories of childhood? Are there any sad ones? Which people had the most influence on your life when you were small? In what ways?

2 Read this extract from a poem by Carol Ann Duffy.

> You could travel up the Blue Nile
> with your finger, tracing the route
> while Mrs Tilscher chanted the scenery.
> Tana. Ethiopia. Khartoum. Aswan.

From In Mrs Tilscher's Class

What is the situation? Who is speaking? What kind of poetry is this? Quickly read the text about Carol Ann Duffy to check your answers.

3 Read the text again and answer these questions.
1 What was Carol Ann Duffy's family background?
2 When were her first works published?
3 What did she study at university?
4 Which of her poems first become famous?
5 How many collections of her poems have been published?
6 How does the text explain 'dramatic monologue'?
7 What does 'placed on the school syllabus' mean?
8 Which honours has she received?

4 During her career, what different kinds of work, e.g. scriptwriter, has Carol Ann Duffy done? What does each job involve?

Carol Ann Duffy

Dame Carol Ann Duffy was born to a working-class Catholic family in Glasgow in 1955. When she was 14 she decided she wanted to be a poet, and two years later *Outposts*, a leading poetry magazine, published some of her poems. After obtaining a degree in philosophy, she worked as a scriptwriter for television, a freelance writer and a poetry editor. She is also highly regarded as a playwright.

In 1983 she won the National Poetry Competition with *Whoever She Was*, and then the Scottish Arts Council Award for her first full collection of poetry. Since then she has had five further collections published. Many of her poems are in the form of a dramatic monologue, which is rather like a speech from a play: a character speaks, giving clues to the sort of person they are, who they are speaking to, and the situation.

In 1994 her poetry was placed on the school syllabus for England and Wales, and her work continues to be widely studied in British schools. She was appointed Poet Laureate in 2009, the first woman to hold the position. She was named a Dame Commander of the British Empire in 2015.

5 Read this complete poem by Carol Ann Duffy and decide who is speaking:

A a parent

B a child

C a grown-up child

D a friend of a child

6 Find words and phrases in the poem with these meanings.

1 something you can't see or remember clearly

2 nobody really knows

3 asked in a very emotional way

4 controlled the situation

5 able to make better decisions because of age

6 strong and in control

7 resulted in you crying

We Remember Your Childhood Well

Nobody hurt you. Nobody turned off the light and argued
with somebody else all night. The bad man on the moors
was only a movie you saw. Nobody locked the door.

Your questions were answered fully. No. That didn't occur.
You couldn't sing anyway, cared less. The moment's a blur, a Film Fun
laughing itself to death in the coal fire. Anyone's guess.

Nobody forced you. You wanted to go that day. Begged. You chose
the dress. Here are the pictures, look at you. Look at us all,
smiling and waving, younger. The whole thing is inside your head.

What you recall are impressions; we have the facts. We called the tune.
The secret police of your childhood were older and wiser than you, bigger
than you. Call back the sound of their voices. Boom. Boom. Boom.

Nobody sent you away. That was an extra holiday, with people
you seemed to like. They were firm, there was nothing to fear.
There was none but yourself to blame if it ended in tears.

What does it matter now? No, no, nobody left the skidmarks of sin
on your soul and laid you wide open for Hell. You were loved.
Always. We did what was best. We remember your childhood well.

7 Answer these questions about the poem.

1 Who is the speaker talking to? Why does the speaker use the plural form 'we'? What is the significance of the title?

2 What is the speaker trying to do? Why is he or she doing this? Is his/her argument convincing? How do you think the other person feels?

3 In what way are the opening lines of all the stanzas similar? What does this indicate about the relationship between the people? What effect does the repeated use of words like *nobody* and *no* give?

4 Why, according to the speaker, does the other person see things differently? How does that person probably feel about their life now?

5 Which frightening images and events, for a child, are used in the poem?

6 Which part of the fourth stanza uses onomatopoeia (words with sounds like the noise they describe)?

7 What do you notice about the length of sentences used? What does this convey?

8 What kinds of rhyme are there? Which words rhyme with: *occur, less, tune, fears, Hell*?

9 Why do you think the title is repeated at the end of the poem?

What do you think?

• How do you think the grown-up child would feel about being spoken to like this?

• Do you think the parents are trying to deny what really happened, that the child has made it all up, or that the reality of what happened lies somewhere between the two? Why?

• Does this poem support the idea that parents 'know better' than their children? In what ways could both parents and children benefit from reading and thinking about this poem?

PROJECT

Think back to your own childhood and try to remember as much detail as you can about an event which has stayed in your memory. Make notes on the event and then write two paragraphs about it: one from your point of view as a child, the other from your parents' point of view. Think about:

• where it happened and how old you were then

• what happened and how you felt at the time

• what your parents said or did about it

• why you still remember it well

1 Which cities in your country have an underground rail system? Have you ever travelled on it, or on the system in another country? How did you feel about it?

2 The title of the text below is a warning given on some stations in the London Underground. What do you think it means? Read the text to check your answer.

MIND THE GAP!

The London Underground is the world's oldest underground system and covers most of Greater London. Although it is called the Underground, about 55% of the network is actually above ground.

It has 270 stations and 11 interconnecting lines. Each line has a name and a colour to represent it on the underground map, for example the Victoria Line is blue. The London Underground is also one of the longest underground systems in the world, with over 400 kilometres of track. Its first passenger trains started running in 1863, on the Metropolitan Line, and today 4.8 million passengers travel on it every day. Londoners call the Underground the Tube, after its tube-shaped tunnels.

During the Blitz, the aerial bombing of London in World War II, Londoners hid from the bombs by using the underground stations as shelters during air raids and slept on platforms overnight. Air-raid sirens were a signal of approaching planes and for Londoners to go down to the stations.

The Underground runs 24 hours a day on certain lines at weekends, but normally the first trains start operating shortly after 5 a.m., running until around 1 a.m.; rush hour is from 7.30 to 9.30 in the morning and 4.30 to 6.30 in the evening.

London is divided into six travel zones. Zone one is the most central zone and zone six is the outer zone which includes Heathrow Airport. The more zones you cross, the more you pay on the Underground. To travel on the Underground, you can buy a daily ticket, a daily travel card, or an Oyster card. This is a smart card with an electronic chip that you charge with credit, and use to pay for travel on the Underground and on buses. It is the cheapest way of travelling in central London.

Some Underground stations have lifts; most have escalators and stairs. The longest escalator in Europe is at Angel station on the Northern Line: it is 60 metres in length, with a vertical rise of 27.5 metres. In nearly all stations people using the escalators stand on the right-hand side, so those in a hurry can walk past them on the left.

There are several safety announcements given to passengers who travel on the Underground. When the doors of the trains are about to close, you hear 'Stand clear of the doors, please'. When the train stops in a station where there is a gap between the train and the platform you will hear the famous phrase, 'Mind the Gap!'.

3 Read the text again carefully. Are these statements True (*T*) or False (*F*)?

1 Most of the Underground is below the surface of London.
2 Victoria Line stations are all painted blue.
3 The Underground is used by three million people a day.
4 When London was being bombed during the Second World War, people slept in the Underground.
5 The Underground is open 24 hours a day, seven days a week.
6 You pay the same amount to travel any distance on the Underground.
7 To use an Oyster card, you have to pay before you travel.
8 Usually people who are not walking up or down the escalators should stand on the left.

4 Complete the crossword with words from the text.

Across

1 time when many people are going to or from work (2 words)
4 people who are travelling by train
7 one every day
8 Underground route
10 metal lines that trains travel on
12 area of the city
13 long hole under the ground

Down

2 place where trains stop
3 upward movement
5 complete system of Underground lines
6 moving stairs that take people up and down
8 machine that carries people straight up or down
9 local name for the London Underground
11 make journeys

5 The BBC TV programme *Top Gear* held a race across London using four means of transport: car, boat, bicycle and Tube. Which do you think won? Find out by reading this review of the programme.

Top Gear: The race across London

The traffic in London, as those of us who live here know only too well, is at an almost permanent standstill, so the BBC TV motoring programme *Top Gear* organized a race to discover the fastest way of getting across the city: from West London to City Airport in the east.

Each of the four presenters was given a different means of transport. James, the posh one, opted for a car – though quite why he chose a giant Mercedes GL500 remains a mystery; Richard, the cute one, who survived that horrific high-speed accident on a car-testing circuit, wisely went for a bicycle this time; Jeremy, true to form, decided on a powerful speedboat to use on the Thames; while the show's pet racing driver, 'The Stig', who turned up for the event in full Formula 1 gear, was given … an Oyster card.

The result must have been a shock for many of the petrol-head viewers of *Top Gear*. By the time Jeremy came charging into the airport, Richard was already sitting comfortably in the first-class lounge. 'The Stig', after receiving some curious looks on the Underground, was third. And James's luxury, gas-guzzling car came in a thoroughly deserved last.

6 Answer the questions about the text.

1 What do you think 'at an almost permanent standstill' means?
2 Who is James? Why did he decide to cross London in a big car?
3 Why do you think the text says Richard 'wisely' chose to ride a bicycle?
4 How was 'The Stig' dressed?
5 What do you think 'petrol-head' means? Why would these viewers be shocked by the result of the race?
6 What do you think 'gas-guzzling' means? Why did James deserve to come last?

What do you think?

- Did the outcome of this race make any useful points? What would be the result of a similar race in the capital city of your country? Are there any other considerations, apart from speed?
- Would you be in favour of charging drivers every time they enter a city? Should we completely ban motor vehicles from city centres?

PROJECT

Think about the public transport system in your city, or another city that you know well. Use the Internet, newspapers and magazines to gather information about it, and write a guide (in about 150 words) for English-speaking visitors.

John McCrae – *In Flanders Fields*

1 Where did the events in the first picture take place? What does the picture on page 37 show?

2 Read the text about the war poet John McCrae. Which two things did he become most famous for?

3 Read the text again and answer the questions.

1 Was *In Flanders Fields* written towards the end of the First World War?

2 Did McCrae write it when he was a young soldier?

3 What was his opinion of the poem after he had written it?

4 How did he feel about it being used by governments?

5 Did McCrae die before he became famous?

6 What is Remembrance Day?

7 Why do some people dislike the poem?

8 Who do you think were particularly against conscription?

9 Was McCrae the first to connect poppies with war?

10 How are poppies used to commemorate the fallen these days?

4 Match the bold words in the text with these meanings.

1 act of putting a dead body into the ground

2 without their name being made public

3 soldiers

4 join the army, navy or air force

5 said aloud from memory

6 take place to make people remember an important event

7 show great public respect for

8 criticizes

9 information or ideas that may be exaggerated or false

10 law making people join the army, navy or air force

11 died

12 people who have served in the army, navy or air force in wartime

JOHN McCRAE

It was nine months into the First World War of 1914–18 when Lieutenant-Colonel John McCrae, a Canadian Army doctor serving in the Flanders region of Belgium, conducted the **burial** of his friend Lieutenant Alexis Helmer. The next day, with scenes of death and destruction all around him, he was inspired to write his most famous poem: *In Flanders Fields*.

A poet since his student days at the University of Toronto in the early 1890s, McCrae was initially dissatisfied with his latest work and is believed to have thrown the poem away, only for it to be found by fellow soldiers. They encouraged him to have it published, which eventually he did, **anonymously**, in London in December 1915.

In Flanders Fields quickly became popular with Canadian soldiers and civilians, as well as those in other English-speaking countries. **Troops** in Belgium would ask him for handwritten copies once they realized who had written it. It was translated into many languages and parts of it were used on government posters to encourage young men to **enlist** and fight, and also to help raise money for the war effort. McCrae himself was both surprised and pleased by this.

John McCrae did not live to see the end of the war: he died of pneumonia in January 1918. His poetry, though, lived on. Each year *In Flanders Fields* is **recited** at ceremonies around the world – especially in Commonwealth countries – on Remembrance Day, which is held every November 11th to **commemorate** the end

of the First World War and **honour** the dead of all wars. In his own country many people believe it should be the national poem, and until recently there was an extract from it on the Canadian $10 bill.

Not everyone, however, admires the poem. Critics claim the final stanza encourages war and **reproaches** those seeking peace, and that through its use as government **propaganda** it may even have helped prolong the First World War. In Canada in 1917, politicians used it in a successful campaign to introduce **conscription**, bitterly opposed by many Canadians. Nevertheless, McCrae remains widely respected in Canada and elsewhere, with a museum named after him at his birthplace in Guelph, Ontario, and an *In Flanders Fields* Museum in Ypres, Belgium.

Possibly McCrae's most significant achievement was the popularization of the poppy as an international symbol of remembrance for fallen soldiers. Although these red flowers had long been associated with war, it was in the soil of the Flanders battlefields where they grew particularly quickly above the graves of those who had **perished**. In 1921, inspired by the words of *In Flanders Fields*, the American Legion adopted it as a symbol to honour their dead in the First World War, soon to be followed by **veterans'** groups throughout the British Empire. Nowadays, artificial poppies are worn before and during Remembrance Day by many people in Britain and in other Commonwealth countries.

5 Read *In Flanders Fields*. Then read the poem again to answer the questions.

1 How does the poem rhyme?

2 Which two lines have a different rhyme? Why do you think the poet did this?

3 Every line has either eight or four syllables. Which syllables are stressed? Underline these. What kind of rhythm does this give the poem?

4 Find examples in the poem of alliteration: the repeated use of the same letter and sound, particularly at the beginning of words.

6 Match the words from the poem with the meanings below.

> larks scarce amid glow quarrel foe
> failing torch ye faith

1 you _____

2 light that can be carried _____

3 fight _____

4 trust _____

5 almost not _____

6 enemy _____

7 birds that sing beautifully _____

8 in the middle of _____

9 losing strength _____

10 produce light _____

7 Answer the questions about the poem.

1 What do the 'crosses' in line 2 mark?

2 Whose voice is speaking in the poem? Which word in line 3 tells you?

3 What can just be heard, despite the noise from the guns?

4 Which other features of the natural world does the poet mention? Why does he do this?

5 How old do you think 'the dead' (line 6) were when they died?

6 Who are the dead speaking to?

7 What does 'the torch' on line 12 symbolize?

8 What do the dead want the living to do? What will happen if the living don't do this?

9 Do you think this poem is anti-war, pro-war or neither? Why?

10 How do you feel about the poem being used as propaganda by governments?

In Flanders Fields

1 In Flanders fields the poppies blow
Between the crosses, row on row,
That mark our place; and in the sky
The larks, still bravely singing, fly
5 Scarce heard amid the guns below.

We are the Dead. Short days ago
We lived, felt dawn, saw sunset glow,
Loved and were loved, and now we lie
In Flanders fields.

10 Take up our quarrel with the foe;
To you from failing hands we throw
The torch; be yours to hold it high.
If ye break faith with us who die
We shall not sleep, though poppies grow
15 In Flanders fields.

What do you think?

- Do you think people should commemorate those who die fighting for their country? Why? / Why not?
- How do you think the men who fought in 1914–18 felt about the war? If you had been of military age at the time, would you have been willing to fight?
- Should governments ever be able to make young people go to war? Why? / Why not?
- In what ways are today's wars different from the First World War?
- Which conflicts are 'just wars', i.e. morally right, and which are not? Why?

PROJECT

Think about what was happening in your country during the First World War. Use the Internet, history textbooks and/or encyclopaedias to find out more about the lives of people at war or under occupation at the time. Imagine you were there at the time, and write a diary entry describing what you saw, heard and felt.

11 LITERATURE

Sir Arthur Conan Doyle – *The Hound of the Baskervilles*

1 Work in pairs. Write a list of famous detectives in fiction, the cinema or on television. Compare your list with your partner.

2 Read the text about Sir Arthur Conan Doyle. What were Conan Doyle's other interests apart from writing Sherlock Holmes stories?

Elementary, my dear Watson!

Sir Arthur Ignatius Conan Doyle was a Scottish writer who wrote detective stories, plays, historical novels, science fiction, and non-fiction. He was born in Edinburgh, Scotland, on 22nd May 1859. He attended boarding school in England, and although he was unhappy there, he was very popular with the other students because of his talent for telling amazing stories. After leaving school in 1875, he studied medicine at Edinburgh University, where he began writing short stories. After university he became a ship's doctor and travelled to the West African coast. In 1882, he returned to the United Kingdom and worked as a doctor in Plymouth before setting up his own medical practice in Southsea.

At the same time, Conan Doyle began to establish himself as a writer. He wrote several historical novels, but it was with the detective novel *A Study in Scarlet*, whose two main characters were Sherlock Holmes and his assistant Dr Watson, that he found his greatest success. When he moved his medical practice to London, not a single patient entered his consulting room, and he used the time to write a series of short stories featuring Sherlock Holmes. The stories were first published as a serial in *The Strand Magazine*, and were hugely popular. However, Conan Doyle felt that he should be writing more serious literature, and decided to kill off Sherlock Holmes, saying that, 'he takes my mind from better things'. In 1893, in the story *The Final Problem*, Sherlock Holmes and his enemy Professor Moriarty both died in Switzerland. Sherlock Holmes fans were furious, and 20,000 readers cancelled their subscription to the magazine.

After an unsuccessful attempt to enter politics, Conan Doyle decided to write one more Sherlock Holmes story, which was set in an earlier period than *The Final Problem*, and this became *The Hound of the Baskervilles*, which was a great success. After being knighted by King Edward VII, who was a Sherlock Holmes fan, Conan Doyle brought his character back to life and wrote a new series of stories for *The Strand Magazine*, called *The Return of Sherlock Holmes*.

As well as writing detective fiction, Conan Doyle took an interest in real cases of injustice, and two men were released from prison because he proved, in a Sherlock Holmes style, that they could not have committed the crimes. After this, the Court of Criminal Appeal was established in 1907 to ensure that other miscarriages of justice could be corrected.

3 Find the words 1–10 in the text and match them to their definitions a–j.

1	historical novels	6	subscription	
2	science fiction	7	set	
3	non-fiction	8	miscarriages of justice	
4	main characters	9	translated	
5	serial	10	adapted	

a the money you pay every year to receive copies of a magazine
b when courts find innocent people guilty
c books about real people and events
d rewritten in a different language
e stories written in a period in the past
f a story published in different parts
g changed so that it works as a film
h with the action taking place in a particular place and time
i the most important people in the story
j stories about life in the future

4 Read the text again. Are these sentences True (*T*) or False (*F*)? Correct the false sentences.

1 Conan Doyle wrote short stories at school.
2 *A Study in Scarlet* was his first novel.
3 Conan Doyle found great success as a doctor.
4 Conan Doyle stopped writing Sherlock Holmes stories because he wanted to concentrate on medicine.
5 Conan Doyle tried to become a politician.
6 Sherlock Holmes managed to release two men from prison.
7 Conan Doyle's most famous line is 'Elementary, my dear Watson!'.

After spending the last part of his life studying spiritualism, Conan Doyle died aged 71 on 7th July 1930. He is buried in Hampshire, England. The Sherlock Holmes stories have been translated into many languages, and adapted for theatre and film. It is the films, not the Sherlock Holmes stories themselves, which produced the famous line 'Elementary, my dear Watson!', which people still sometimes say when they think a problem is easy to solve.

5 *The Hound of the Baskervilles* is set on the moors of Dartmoor, near where Conan Doyle was a doctor in Plymouth. It was originally a serial in *The Strand Magazine* from 1901 to 1902. In the story, Sherlock Holmes and Dr Watson are called to investigate a *curse over the house of the Baskerville family. Read an extract from the story. What have people seen on the moor?

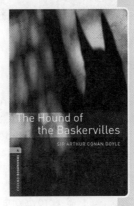

* a word or phrase that has the power to make bad things happen

6 Find words in the extract which mean … .

1 open, rough, windy land, usually on hills and without trees
2 a kind of dog used for catching wild animals
3 the spirit of a person or animal that appears after they have died
4 a large country house
5 to pull something into pieces
6 marks on the ground made by feet or shoes
7 people who are qualified to advise people about the law
8 the front part of the neck, which food goes down
9 practical and rational

7 Read the extract again and answer the questions.

1 Why was Sherlock Holmes angry?
2 Why are the people frightened?
3 Why does Sherlock Holmes think the animal isn't a ghost?
4 Who is Sir Henry?
5 Why has Dr Mortimer asked Sherlock Holmes for help?
6 What does Sherlock Holmes suggest?

> ### What do you think?
>
> * Do you like detective stories? Why / Why not? Why do you think they are so popular?
> * Who is your favourite detective in fiction?
> * What is the typical sequence of events in a classic detective story?

> ### PROJECT
>
> Write a review in about 150 words for a website selling books and DVDs, of a detective story you have read, or a TV series or film featuring a detective.
>
> **Include information about:**
> * the author
> * the setting
> * the characters
> * the detective
> * the plot

The Problem

'Sir Charles had left his footprints all over that little bit of the path where he was standing. I couldn't see any other prints.'

Sherlock Holmes hit his knee with his hand angrily. 'I like to look closely at these things myself,' he said. 'Oh, Dr Mortimer, why didn't you call me immediately?'

'Mr Holmes, the best detective in the world can't help with some things,' said Mortimer.

'You mean things that are outside the laws of nature – supernatural things?' asked Holmes.

'I didn't say so exactly,' replied Mortimer. 'But since Sir Charles died, I have heard about a number of things that seem to be supernatural. Several people have seen an animal on the moor that looks like an enormous hound. They all agree that it was a huge creature, which shone with a strange light like a ghost. I have questioned these people carefully. They are all sensible people. They all tell the same story. Although they have only seen the creature far away, it is exactly like the hell-hound of the Baskerville story. The people are very frightened, and only the bravest man will cross the moor at night.'

'And you, a man of science, believe that the creature is supernatural – something from another world?' asked Holmes.

'I don't know what to believe,' said Dr Mortimer.

'But you must agree that the footprints were made by a living creature, not a ghost?'

'When the hound first appeared two hundred and fifty years ago, it was real enough to tear out Sir Hugo's throat … . But it was a supernatural hell-hound,' said Dr Mortimer.

'If you think that Sir Charles' death was caused by something supernatural, my detective work can't help you,' said Holmes, rather coldly.

'Perhaps,' said Mortimer. 'But you can help me by advising me what to do for Sir Henry Baskerville. He arrives in London by train in exactly', Dr Mortimer looked at his watch, 'one hour and a quarter.'

'Sir Henry is now head of the Baskerville family?' asked Holmes.

'Yes,' said Dr Mortimer. 'He is the last of the Baskervilles. The family lawyers contacted him in the USA. He has come to England immediately by ship. He landed this morning. Now, Mr Holmes, what do you advise me to do with him?'

'Why should he not go to the family home?' asked Holmes.

'Because so many Baskervilles who go there die horrible deaths. But Sir Charles' good work must go on. If it doesn't, all the people on the Baskerville lands will be much poorer. If the Baskerville family leaves the Hall, that is what will happen. I don't know what to do. This is why I came to you for advice.'

Holmes thought for a little while. Then he said: 'You think it is too dangerous for any Baskerville to live at the Hall because of this supernatural hell-hound. Well, I think you should go and meet Sir Henry Baskerville. Say nothing to him about this. I shall give you my advice in twenty-four hours. At ten o'clock tomorrow morning, Dr Mortimer, I would like you to bring Sir Henry Baskerville here.'

[Extract taken from: Oxford Bookworms stage 4, The Hound of the Baskervilles]

12A

The American Revolution

1 How much do you know about the early history of the United States of America? Choose the correct alternative.

1 Britain established its first colony in North America in the *17th / 18th Century*.

2 The American War of Independence started in *1775 / 1785*.

3 *Twelve / Thirteen* colonies originally formed the United States of America.

4 Independence Day is celebrated on *June 4th / July 4th*.

5 The first American president was *Thomas Jefferson / George Washington*.

2 Read the text about the American Revolution and check your answers.

3 Match the words from the text to their definitions.

1	consulted	a	given natural possession of
2	representation	b	free to govern itself
3	cargo	c	that cannot be taken away
4	escalated	d	equal
5	provisional	e	became more serious
6	egalitarian	f	not permanent
7	endowed	g	the goods carried on a ship
8	inalienable	h	asked for an opinion
9	mercenaries	i	people to speak for you
10	sovereign	j	soldiers who will fight for anyone who pays

THE AMERICAN REVOLUTION

Britain established several colonies in North America during the 17th Century, starting with Virginia in 1607, and in the mid-18th Century the British government decided to tax its American colonies more strictly. The problem for many American colonists was not that taxes were high, but that the colonies were not consulted about them, as they had no representation in Parliament. The popular slogan 'No taxation without representation!' reflected growing unrest amongst the people, and there were many political debates about the role of democracy and republican values in society.

In 1773, the British government passed the Tea Act, which made it easier for the British East India Tea company to import cheaper tea into America, using their own agents and **cutting out** the local American agents completely. When three British ships carrying tea docked in Boston harbour in December of that year, about 150 Americans, poorly disguised as Native Americans, **boarded** the ships and threw all 342 chests of their precious cargo into the sea – an event now referred to as 'The Boston Tea Party'.

From that point on, many Americans came to see tea drinking as unpatriotic and turned to coffee instead. Today, visitors to the floating Tea Party Museum in Boston can explore **replicas** of two of the original ships, see one of the actual tea chests – and throw tea overboard.

As protests and violence escalated further around Boston, groups of local **militia** began to form, and British soldiers were sent to nearby Lexington to **confiscate** a store of weapons. As British soldiers faced the colonial rebels, the 'shot heard around the world' was fired on April 19th 1775, and the American War of Independence had begun. The thirteen colonies involved formed a provisional government called 'The United Colonies of America', and formed their own 'Continental Army' under the leadership of George Washington. They declared their independence on July 4th 1776, a date which is still celebrated with a national holiday every year on the 4th July, Independence Day.

The Declaration of Independence, written by Thomas Jefferson, was influenced by the Enlightenment philosophy that had come out of Europe, and shows the desire for a new, more **egalitarian** society. Its opening lines have become famous: *We hold these truths to be self-evident, that all men are created equal, that they are endowed by their Creator with certain inalienable Rights, that among these are Life, Liberty and the pursuit of Happiness.*

The British suffered some surprise defeats at the hands of the Continental Army, but returned to the war with reinforcements (25% of them German mercenaries). The Americans formed an alliance with France in 1778, and the French helped them with money, weapons and ships. Among the many French soldiers who fought for the Americans was the Marquis de Lafayette, promoted to the rank of Major General at the age of just 19. The war ended with the Treaty of Paris in 1783 and the United States became a sovereign state, with George Washington as its first President.

4 Work out the meaning of the bold words in the text from their context.

1 cutting out   3 replicas   5 confiscate
2 boarded   4 militia   6 egalitarian

5 Read the text again and answer the questions.

1 Why did Britain decide to tax its American colonies more strictly?
2 Why were the taxes so unpopular with the American colonies?
3 When did the Boston Tea Party take place?
4 Why did the British soldiers go to Lexington?
5 Who declared their independence on July 4th 1776?
6 In what way was the Declaration of Independence both very modern and very old-fashioned?
7 How did France help the Americans during the American War of Independence?
8 When did the American War of Independence end?

6 Read these paragraphs about the first and the 45th US Presidents.
What differences and similarities are there between the two men?

George Washington was born to a prosperous family in 1732 in what was then the British colony of Virginia. He was an experienced soldier and led the Americans to victory in the War of Independence. He was the first President of the United States from 1789–1797, the only President to ever receive 100% of the electoral votes. Washington laid down the foundations of many important values and principles, although – like many rich landowners of the time – he also owned African-American slaves. He made sure that America did not interfere in European politics and that other countries did not influence domestic affairs. Washington DC, the capital city of the USA, is named after him.

Donald Trump, whose father was a wealthy property developer, was born in New York City in 1946. As a teenager he attended the New York Military Academy but was not drafted during the Vietnam War. He extended his father's property business, becoming a billionaire in the process, and was the star of the TV show *The Apprentice*. In 2016 he unexpectedly became the 45th President of the United States by obtaining 57% of the electoral votes, despite losing the popular vote to Hillary Clinton. During the campaign he was widely criticized for his comments about women and ethnic minorities, but also received support for his promises to reduce the United States' international commitments and to 'Make America Great Again'.

What do you think?

- Do you know the names of the two US presidents before Donald Trump? What is each of them remembered for?
- Do you think recent Presidents of the United States have followed George Washington's thinking about involvement in international affairs? Why / Why not?
- In what ways has America colonized the rest of the world culturally?

PROJECT

Write a paragraph with a description of the American flag, the Stars and Stripes, for a guide to American culture. Use the Internet to help you. Include information on:
- the colour and design
- what the stars and stripes represent
- when it was adopted

The Fascinating Diary of Samuel Pepys

1 Do you or does anyone you know keep a diary? What things do you / they write in it? Do you think these diaries will be interesting for historians to read in 400 years' time?

2 Between 1660 and 1669, Samuel Pepys wrote a unique diary that brings to life the great events of that time in London. Read his biography. Find words or phrases in the text that mean 1–5 below.

1 regularly wrote
2 wrote down
3 a secret way of writing information
4 a description of an event by someone who saw it
5 the section of one particular day in a diary

3 Read the text again and answer the questions.

1 What did Pepys do to see the king's execution?
2 When did Pepys write his diary?
3 What was the Restoration period in England?
4 Name some historical events that Pepys wrote about in his diary.
5 When did Pepys stop writing the diary? Why?
6 Why did it take so long to publish a full version of the diary?
7 Where is Pepys' diary now?

4 Look at the entries from Samuel Pepys' diaries. Read them. Which entries **A–D** refer to . . . ?

1 the Great Plague (x2)
2 his daily life
3 the Great Fire of London

Samuel Pepys

Samuel Pepys (pronounced /piːps/) was born in London in 1633, and was the son of a tailor. At the age of 15, he and some friends played truant from school to watch the public beheading of King Charles I. After graduating from Cambridge University in 1654 he went on to become Chief Secretary to the Admiralty under King James II.

He is famous for the very detailed private diary he kept during the years 1660–1669. In some ways it is a very ordinary diary – he recorded details of his daily life, work and relationships with women, which is probably why the diary is written in a code that included the use of Spanish, French and Italian words. But it is also an important historical document about the Restoration period in England (when the monarchy was restored, after a period of republican rule under the military leader Oliver Cromwell). He includes fascinating eyewitness accounts of events in 17th Century England, for example the Great Plague in 1665 (also known as the Black Death, which killed thousands of people), and the Great Fire of London in 1666.

He wrote the last entry in his diary on 31st May 1669, because he could no longer see properly. Pepys died in 1703, leaving strict instructions that all his writings were to be kept in the library at Magdalene College, Cambridge. There the diary remained until the 19th century, when an attempt was made to decode it without the key. Eventually the key was discovered and parts of the diary were published, but many of the details of Pepys' private life were considered too shocking for Victorian readers and it was not until the 1970s – three centuries after it was written – that a complete edition came out. The original diary of Samuel Pepys is still housed at Magdalene College, and it can also be read in the form of a daily blog at pepysdiary.com.

A _____   *1660 January 16th*

... we went towards Westminster on foot, and at the Golden Lion, near Charing Cross, we went in and drank a pint of wine, and so parted; and *thence home, where I found my wife and maid a-washing. I *staid up till the bell-man came by with his bell, just under my window as I was writing of this very line, and cried, "Past one of the clock, and a cold, frosty, windy morning." I then went to bed and left my wife and the maid a-washing still.

* *thence* – then   * *staid* – old spelling of 'stayed'

B _____   *1665 June 7th*

This day, much against my will, I did in Drury Lane see two or three houses marked with a red cross upon the doors, and "Lord have mercy upon us" *write there; which was a sad sight to me, being the first of the kind that, to my remembrance, I ever saw.

* *write* – written

C _____   *1665 August 31st*

In the City died this week 7,496 and of them 6,102 of the plague. But it is feared that the true number of the dead this week is near 10,000; partly from the poor that cannot be taken notice of through the greatness of the number, and partly from the *Quakers and others that will not have *nay bell ring for them.

* *Quakers* – a Christian religious group   * *nay* – (not) any

---

7 Read the text about the Great Fire of London. In what ways was the fire a disaster? What were the fire's positive effects for London? Do you think these outweigh the harm done at the time? Why / Why not?

D _____
1666 September 2nd (Lord's day).

By and by Jane comes and tells me that she hears that above 300 houses have been burned down to-night by the fire we saw, and that it is now burning down all Fish-street, by London Bridge. So I made myself ready presently, and walked to the Tower, and there got up upon one of the high places, Sir J. Robinson's little son going up with me; and there I did see the houses at that end of the bridge all on fire, and an infinite great fire on this and the other side the end of the bridge … So down, with my heart full of trouble, to the Lieutenant of the Tower, who tells me that it begun this morning in the King's baker's house in Pudding-lane, and that it *hath burned St. Magnus's Church and most part of Fish-street already. So I down to the water-side, and there got a boat and through bridge, and there saw a *lamentable fire. … Everybody endeavouring to remove their goods, and flinging into the river or bringing them into *lighters that *lay off; poor people staying in their houses as long as till the very fire touched them, and then running into boats, or clambering from one pair of stairs by the water-side to another.

* *hath* – has   * *lamentable* – terrible   * *lighters* – small, flat boats
* *lay off* – were nearby

5 Match the words from the diary entries with their definitions.

1	maid	a	throwing something in a careless way
2	presently	b	attempting to do something
3	infinite	c	an officer in the army or navy
4	Lieutenant	d	a female servant in a house or a hotel
5	endeavouring	e	in a short time
6	flinging	f	moving with difficulty, using your hands and feet
7	clambering	g	without limits

6 Read the entries again and answer the questions.

1 What time did Pepys go to bed in entry A?
2 What sign did people put on their door to show they had the plague?
3 How many people in London died of the plague during the week of 31st August 1665?
4 Where did Pepys go to watch the fire of London?
5 Where did the Great Fire of London start?
6 What did Londoners do to try and escape from the fire?

The Great Fire of London started in a bakery in 1666 in Pudding Lane near London Bridge. Eighty per cent of the City of London was destroyed in the fire, including 13,000 houses and 87 churches. The fire lasted for three days, but amazingly only nine people died in it! One good thing that came out of the fire of London was that it eliminated London's brown rat population, which carried the Great Plague that had killed about 100,000 Londoners in 1665. The first insurance company in the world (Lloyds of London) was started after the Great Fire, as people began to realize the importance of insurance against natural disaster. The Great Fire burnt down all of London's medieval wooden buildings and gave the King, Charles II, the opportunity to build new, safer stone buildings.

In 1677, to remember the Great Fire of London, Sir Christopher Wren, a famous English architect designed the Monument. It is a column of stone which is 202ft (61.57m) high. When it was built, it was the tallest stone column in the world. It is situated near to London Bridge, very close to where the fire started. There are 311 stairs and visitors who climb up the Monument are given a certificate on their way out to show they reached the top!

What do you think?

• What effect might seeing a public execution have on a 15-year-old?
• Pepys wrote his diary in code so that anyone who found it would find it difficult to read. If you found a diary belonging to a family member or a friend, would you read some of the entries? Why / Why not?

PROJECT

Does your town or a town near where you live have a monument to an event in history? Write a tourist factfile about it. Include the following information.

• Where is it exactly?
• When was it built?
• Who built it?
• Why was it built?
• What does it look like?

Glossary

1A The British Empire

legacy something that is left to you from an earlier period

to set (the sun) to go down at the end of the day

to rule over to be in control of

to extend to to go as far as

at its peak when it was biggest

expanded got bigger

mariner sailor

the globe the earth

penal colonies places in other countries that were used as prisons

benefited from got a good result from

reliant on depending on

harvests the results from collecting the food you have grown

disputes arguments

1B Sujata Bhatt – *Search for My Tongue*

synonymous with the same thing as

repercussions many different results

heritage the culture that you get from your parents and country

explicitly clearly and exactly

implications suggested connections

conveyed expressed

synthesis mixture

inflections changes in how high or low the voice is

dual having two parts

to rot to go bad, like food that is old

to spit out to make something come out of your mouth

stump the short part that is left when something is cut off

a shoot the new part of a plant that grows out of the ground

veins the tubes that carry blood in your body, and sap in a plant

bud the small lump on a plant that opens into a flower

to blossom to open into a flower

2A The BBC

broadcasting making and sending out radio or television programmes

mission the work they believe it is their duty to do

diversity range of people or things that are different from each other

chat shows programmes in which famous people are asked questions and talk in an informal way about their work and opinions

sitcoms 'sitcom' is short for 'situation comedy', a regular programme that shows the same characters in different funny situations

soaps short for 'soap operas', which are stories about the lives and problems of a group of people, broadcast every day or several times a week

consumer shows programmes which focus on the quality and value of products and services

costume dramas plays or series set in the past

current affairs programmes programmes about events of political or social importance that are happening now

wildlife documentaries programmes giving facts about animals, birds, insects, etc. that are wild and live in a natural environment

long-running series sets of programmes that deal with the same subject or that have the same characters, sometimes shown over several years or even decades

household group of people, such as a family, who live together

offence illegal act

prosecution the process of being officially charged with a crime in court

funding providing money for a particular purpose

coverage the reporting of news in the media

unionist someone who believes Northern Ireland, Scotland and/or Wales should remain part of the United Kingdom

cultural connected with the beliefs and attitudes of an organization

bias unfairness in reporting, showing favour to one side

issues important topics that people are discussing or arguing about

satirical using humour to criticize someone or something

impartial not supporting one person or group more than another

2B Queen Elizabeth I

slight small

narrowly escaped only just escaped, nearly didn't escape

secure safe, not likely to fall

compromise an answer to a problem that isn't what either side wanted, but keeps them both happy

expansion getting bigger

flourished grew successfully

thrived were very successful

triumph success, winning

cultivated worked at keeping and developing

threats possibility of danger

temptation something that's difficult to say no to

potential possible

aided helped

a claim the right to say that something belongs to you

severe very bad

drawn pulled

3A Art in the UK – Sir Antony Gormley

murals paintings on walls

collective having the same group character

tide big moving mass, like the sea

infinite never-ending

extend reach

staring looking at someone for a long time

visible possible to see

toiled worked very hard

shift big change

tide the movement of the sea following the moon

waves the parts of the sea that lift up as it reaches land

aim purpose

consumer society society which is only interested in buying things

tribute something that shows you respect someone

knighted given a special honour by a British king or queen

3B The Globe Theatre

playwright person who writes plays

three-storey with three floors (on top of each other)

trap-doors small doors that open to a space under the floor

refreshments food and drinks

commoners ordinary working people

screaming shouting in a high, loud way because you're afraid

nobles people from the aristocracy, the top class of society

masks things you put on your face so people can't see who you are

to hide to stop people from seeing

whispered spoke very quietly

rivalry competition

inferior not as good as

copyright the right to make copies of something

demolished destroyed, knocked down

replica copy

smooth easy; without bumps or difficulties

brief saying something quickly in a few words

tedious boring

nobler of a better character

revenge making someone suffer because they have made you suffer

4A Education in the UK and US

non-selective taking everybody, not only the best

single-sex for only boys, or only girls

syllabus everything that you study in school

fail not succeed

Citizenship how to be a member of society; a school subject

participation saying and doing things, not just sitting quietly

oral spoken

aptitude ability

verbal speaking

to take into account to remember when deciding something

4B Jane Austen – Pride and Prejudice

prejudice negative feelings about people before you really know them

habits things that you always do

to parallel to be similar to

contract a formal agreement to do something, written on paper

to overcome to not let something stop you doing something

to convince to make someone believe they should do something

acknowledged agreed to be true

an objection a reason to not agree to something

fortune a large amount of money

servants people who worked for rich people, doing housework

tiresome boring and annoying

5 Super size America; super size world?

calories the units that show how much energy is in food

overweight too heavy, weighing too much

risen increased

aware of knowing about

to consume to eat

productivity how much is produced by workers

to be aimed at to be directed towards, have the purpose of influencing

rely on depend on

contracts business agreements

instant very quick, immediate

poor not very good

6 Percy Shelley – Ozymandias

exclusive expensive and only for rich or upper-class people

expelled forced to leave

eloped ran away secretly to get married

rift disagreement that harms a relationship

allowance money given regularly

tyranny the cruel and unfair use of power

inspired gave someone an idea for creating something

for good forever

drowned died in the water because it was impossible to breathe

anti-establishment against the people in power in a country

antique very old

trunkless without a body

shattered broken

visage face

frown annoyed look

wrinkled with small lines

sneer look of no respect

mocked made fun of

pedestal base of a statue

mighty powerful

despair lose all hope

decay slow destruction

colossal extremely big

wreck ruined object

boundless without end

stretch continue a long way

7 London West End Theatre

bordered by on every side of

wholly completely

appropriate correct for its use

prior to before

courtyard the open outside area behind a house

spacious with a lot of space to move around in

timber big pieces of wood for building

notion idea

imposing very big and making a strong impression

erected built

maintaining keeping in good condition

to pose a challenge to give you something difficult to do

constant never-ending

exceeded were more than

definitive the best of its kind

prestigious seen as being very important

gender male or female

8A English-speaking capitals

inhabitants the people who live in a place

rivalry competition

roughly about, approximately

weird very strange

seized took control of

massive very big

compromise agreement between people that isn't what either side wanted, but keeps both of them happy

treason doing things against your country

unique the only one that exists

gherkin small cucumber that has been preserved in vinegar

8B Australia: Going to live Down Under

interior the part in the middle

monolith an enormous piece of stone

sacred important for religious reasons

to convert to make people change to a different religion

settled decided to live there permanently

fleet a large group of ships

gold rush when everyone goes to a place because gold has been found

to hunt to go after something in order to kill it

poisoned given things to eat which killed them

restrict to stop the numbers getting too many

illiterate not able to read

poverty not having enough money

waves periods when large numbers come at the same time

9A Teenage Britain

freely admit are happy to say that it's true

self-destructive hurting yourself

set-ups ways of organizing something

substantial a lot of, a significant amount

outcomes results

severely very badly

threaten to say you will hurt someone

embarrass to make someone feel stupid in public

subjected to made to experience

upsetting making you feel very unhappy

9B Carol Ann Duffy – *We Remember Your Childhood Well*

tracing following on a map

scriptwriter person who writes the words for TV dramas, films, etc.

freelance working for yourself, not for an organization

clues things that help you to find the answer to a problem

highly regarded thought to be of very high quality

moors wild, open area of land, with no trees

recall remember

impressions things that you imagine to be true

to blame to say that someone is responsible for bad things happening

skidmarks the black marks on the road where a car tried to stop before crashing

10A Transport in London

covers includes the area of

interconnecting all joined together

air raids when planes drop bombs on an area

sirens the noise to tell people that an air raid is coming

vertical going up

posh from the upper class of society

opted for chose

cute pretty and attractive

true to form as usual

curious wanting to know what is happening

thoroughly completely

10B John McCrae – *In Flanders Fields*

burial act of putting a dead body into the ground

anonymously without their name being made public

troops soldiers

enlist join the army, navy or air force

recited said aloud from memory

commemorate take place to make people remember an important event

honour show great public respect for

reproaches criticizes

propaganda information or ideas that may be exaggerated or false

conscription order making people join the army, navy or air force

perished died

veterans people who have served in the army, navy or air force in wartime

larks birds that sing beautifully

scarce almost not

amid in the middle of

glow produce light

quarrel fight

foe enemy

failing losing strength

torch light that can be carried

ye you

faith trust

11 Sir Arthur Conan Doyle – *The Hound of the Baskervilles*

boarding school   a school where the children live during the school year

to set up   to get started

to establish yourself   to become known

consulting room   the room where doctors see their patients

to cancel   to stop

injustice   when someone is found guilty of a crime they haven't committed

to ensure   to make sure

spiritualism   belief that it's possible to communicate with dead people

huge   very big

to contact   to communicate with

12A The American Revolution

strictly   more carefully, making sure that it happens

slogan   phrase used repeatedly to get people's attention

unrest   unhappiness that is likely to end in angry protest

Act (of parliament)   law

to dock   to arrive (by ship) in a harbour and stay there

disguised as   dressed to look like

desire   a strong wish

self-evident   doesn't need explaining

reinforcements   extra soldiers

alliance   agreement to work together

treaty   a formal agreement

interfere in   to try to influence

domestic affairs   things that are connected with your own country

12B The Fascinating Diary of Samuel Pepys

tailor   a person who makes men's clothes

detailed   with lots of information

restored   brought back to power

plague   a disease that kills a lot of people

to decode   to find the meaning of something written in secret language

parted   left each other

frosty   when thin ice covers everything because it is very cold

much against my will   although I really didn't want to

mercy   forgiving someone instead of punishing them more

goods   things that belong to you

eliminated   made to go away completely

medieval   belonging to the Middle Ages (1000–1450)

column   a tall, circular piece of stone

play truant   stay away from school without permission

beheading   cutting off someone's head, as a punishment

UNIVERSITY PRESS

Great Clarendon Street, Oxford, OX2 6DP, United Kingdom

Oxford University Press is a department of the University of Oxford.
It furthers the University's objective of excellence in research, scholarship,
and education by publishing worldwide. Oxford is a registered trade
mark of Oxford University Press in the UK and in certain other countries

ISBN: 978 0 19 452927 3

Printed in China

This book is printed on paper from certified and well-managed sources

ACKNOWLEDGEMENTS

Back cover photograph: Oxford University Press building/David Fisher

*The authors and publisher are grateful to those who have given permission to reproduce
the following extracts and adaptations of copyright material*: p.6 Extract (adapted)
from the biographical introduction for Sujata Bhatt by Esther Morgan
Copyright © The Poetry Archive, from the poet's page on the Poetry Archive
website at www.poetryarchive.org. p.7 'Search for My Tongue', from Bhatt –
Collected Poems by Sujata Bhatt, September 2013, Carcanet Press Limited.
Reproduced by permission. pp.10–11 'Elizabeth 1', www.royal.gov.uk.
Contains public sector information licensed under the Open Government
Licence v3.0. p.22 Percy Bysshe Shelley (1792–1822) from http://shelleysghost.
bodleian.ox.ac.uk, Bodleian Libraries, University of Oxford. Reproduced by
permission. p.24 'London's Theatreland' from www.officallondontheatre.
co.uk. Reproduced by permission of the Society of London Theatre. p.30
'Unhappy and unfit' by Laura Clark, originally published in Daily Mail
7 August 2006. Reproduced by permission of Solo Syndication. p.33 'We
Remember Your Childhood Well' from The Other Country by Carol Ann
Duffy. Published by Anvil Press Poetry, 1990. Copyright © Carol Ann Duffy.
Reproduced by permission of the author c/o Rogers, Coleridge & White Ltd.,
20 Powis Mews, London W11 1JN. p.39 Oxford Bookworms Stage 4: The Hound
of the Baskervilles by Sir Arthur Conan Doyle, retold by Patrick Nobes. This
simplified edition © Oxford University Press 2008. Reproduced by permission.

The publisher would like to thank the following for permission to reproduce photographs:
123RF p.20 (pizza/Brent Hofacker); Alamy Stock Photo pp.5 (Victoria Memorial,
Calcutta/Eitan Simanor), 6 (Oxford Street/Nathan King), 6 (Sujata Bhatt/M-dash
News Archive), 12 (Another Place sculpture/Chris Deeney), 12 (The Waste
Man/Roger Bamber), 14 (Globe Theatre interior/Peter Phipp/Travelshots.
com), 16 (classroom/Sally and Richard Greenhill), 16 (American classroom/
Martin Shields), 20 (Coca Cola/Steve Stock), 21 (children eating McDonald's/
Alex Segre), 22 (Egyptian ruins/Bygone Collection), 27 (Pretoria park/Images of
Africa Photobank), 27 (the White House/INTERFOTO), 28 (Uluru/David Wall),
28 (kangaroo with joey/Papilio), 30 (youths drinking/John Powell), 36 (John
McCrae/Granger Historical Picture Archive), 41 (George Washington/Classic
Image); Bridgeman Art Library Ltd pp.29 (The immigrants' ship, 1884 (oil on
canvas), Dollman, John Charles (1851–1934)/Art Gallery of South Australia,
Adelaide, Australia), 38 (Portrait of Sir Arthur Conan Doyle (pastel on paper),
Gates, William Henry (1888–1935)/Private Collection), 43 (The Great Fire
of London in 1666, illustration from Hutchinson's 'The Story of the British
Nation', c.1920 (colour litho), Forbes, Stanhope Alexander (1857–1947)/
Private Collection); Getty Images pp.9 (Newsnight/Jeff Overs), 9 (Bengal tiger/
Bengal tiger), 10 (Elizabeth I/Print Collector), 12 (Antony Gormley sculpture/
AFP), 12 (Asian Field, Antony Gormley/JUNG YEON-JE), 13 (Angel of the North/
Robert Lazenby), 22 (Percy Bysshe Shelley/Stock Montage), 25 (The Lion
King theatre/RoBeDeRo), 26 (Canberra/PETER HARRISON), 26 (Bob Marley
Museum/Doug Pearson), 27 (London skyline/Cultura Exclusive/Leon Sosra),
28 (Sydney Opera House/JulieanneBirch), 31 (unhappy teen/Leanne Temme),
40 (American Revolution/Stock Montage), 41 (President Donald Trump/
Mark Wilson), 42 (Samuel Pepys/Bettmann); iStockphoto pp.14 (theatre
masks/stanleystunning), 26 (Ottawa/RonTech2000); Oxford University Press
pp.20 (burger/Davydenko Yuliia), 20 (glass of milk/Mark Mason), 20 (apple/
Mark Mason), 27 (the gherkin/Patrick Wang), 32 (children playing/Photodisc),
32 (happy children/Photodisc), 32 (boy with black eye/Photodisc), 32 (crying
child/Photodisc), 34 (London underground/Image Source), 34 (underground
sign/alice-photo); Press Association Images pp.8 (old television studio/Barratts/
S&G Barratts/EMPICS Archive), 8 (filming/John Stillwell/PA Archive/PA Images);
Rex Shutterstock pp.9 (The Ellen Degeneres Show/NBC-TV/Kobal), 9 (Sense
and Sensibility/Columbia/Kobal), 13 (Witness, Antony Gormley/Glenn Copus/
Evening Standard), 18 (Pride And Prejudice/Moviestore Collection), 35 (Top
Gear presenters/Matt Sadler), 36 (World War I/Hulton Archive); Shutterstock
pp.15 (Globe Theatre/4kclips), 24 (Wicked theatre/Zabotnova Inna), 24 (Harry
Potter theatre/John Gomez), 25 (Romeo and Juliet theatre/Pres Panayotov),
37 (poppy field/A_Lesik).

Illustrations by: Peter Bull pp inside front cover (Map United Kingdom), frontis
page (Map Australia and New Zealand), inside back cover (Map USA and
Canada); Mark Duffin: p.4 (world map); Neil Gower (theatreland map)

Cover photographs: OUP/Shutterstock